**BLACK
BODIES
IN THE
RIVER**

RACE, RHETORIC, AND MEDIA SERIES
Davis W. Houck, General Editor

BLACK BODIES IN THE RIVER

SEARCHING FOR FREEDOM SUMMER

Davis W. Houck

UNIVERSITY PRESS OF MISSISSIPPI / JACKSON

The University Press of Mississippi is the scholarly publishing agency of
the Mississippi Institutions of Higher Learning: Alcorn State University,
Delta State University, Jackson State University, Mississippi State University,
Mississippi University for Women, Mississippi Valley State University,
University of Mississippi, and University of Southern Mississippi.

Designed by Peter D. Halverson

www.upress.state.ms.us

The University Press of Mississippi is a member of
the Association of University Presses.

Portions of this work appeared in altered form in a forum section of
Rhetoric Review 36, no. 4 (2017).

First printing 2022
∞

Library of Congress Cataloging-in-Publication Data

Names: Houck, Davis W., author.
Title: Black bodies in the river : searching for Freedom Summer / Davis W. Houck.
Other titles: Race, rhetoric, and media series.
Description: Jackson : University Press of Mississippi, [2022] | Series: Race, rhetoric, and
media series | Includes bibliographical references and index. |
Identifiers: LCCN 2021061607 (print) | LCCN 2021061608 (ebook) | ISBN 9781496840790
(hardback) | ISBN 9781496840783 (trade paperback) | ISBN 9781496840813 (epub) | ISBN
9781496840806 (epub) | ISBN 9781496840837 (pdf) | ISBN 9781496840820 (pdf)
Subjects: LCSH: Mississippi Freedom Project. | African Americans—Civil rights—Missis-
sippi—History. | Civil rights movements—Mississippi—History—20th century.
Classification: LCC E185.93.M6 H588 2022 (print) | LCC E185.93.M6 (ebook) | DDC
323.1196/07307620904—dc23/eng/20220112
LC record available at https://lccn.loc.gov/2021061607
LC ebook record available at https://lccn.loc.gov/2021061608

British Library Cataloging-in-Publication Data available

CONTENTS

PREFACE

This has been a hard project to complete. So hard in fact that I let it go for several years, content just to let it collect dust on my desk and remain unretrieved on my hard drive. I didn't send it out to colleagues, friends, or family for review. I didn't send anything in for a conference submission. Always there had been an urgency to get my work published, out in the public eye. But save for a quick colloquium in the pages of *Rhetoric Review*, I just ignored it, pretended it didn't really exist. I can't give you a good explanation why.

And then young Black men started dying (again) at the hands of police officers. Weekly, sometimes daily it seemed, video would surface of yet another Black man losing his life at the end of a police-issued pistol. Or a white knee. The excuse always seemed to be the same: "I feared for my life . . ."

In the midst of the latest racial madness a friend called and asked, "Hey, are you ever going to do anything with that Black Bodies in the River manuscript?" I'd let him, and pretty much only him, read it years earlier. At his instigation I dusted the manuscript off, read it again, and decided that it was worthy of a readership, that the cultural moment seemed right to have it participate in a much larger conversation. And so I set about to revise it, update it, and get feedback.

Three people in particular gave this project a lot of their critical energy. Ira Allen at Northern Arizona University didn't rest until he'd read every sentence, every endnote, and raised questions accordingly. He did it the old-fashioned way, not with Microsoft. I had the privilege of teaching him back in 2013, but we both know who's teaching whom these days. Jack Selzer, recently retired from Penn State University's English department, also did some heavy lifting when it came to editing, reading, asking questions, and making suggestions. Jack is a fellow scholar of the movement in Mississippi and an enthusiastic traveler, and I am grateful for his patient counsel. And Mike Hogan, also recently retired from Penn State University and the Communication Arts program: nobody edits my work with his attention to detail. Nobody asks better questions. And so to Ira, Jack, and Mike, thank you.

I had many other superb readers: Wanda Lynn Fenimore, Ray Fleming, Brian Graves, Dave Tell, Devery Anderson, Amos Kiewe, Mary Ealey, Carol Weigle, Ed King, Fowler "Skip" Martin, Kyle Jones, and Beauvais McCaddon each added to what's in these pages. My thanks. As for the many eccentricities that remain, I take full ownership.

The unwieldy story that follows could not have been told well without careful attention to the 1963 Freedom Vote—its aims, how it quickly evolved, its many audiences, and of course its politics; it was a political campaign, after all. Over many years of friendship, the lieutenant governor on that ticket, Rev. Ed King from Jackson, Mississippi, has guided my understanding of that critical five-week campaign in the fall of 1963. Without it, frankly, there is no Summer Project, no Freedom Summer. Rev. King sacrificed a lot to answer Bob Moses's call to create an interracial ticket, a ticket and a platform that Black Mississippians could rally behind and actually vote for. I am humbled to call him a good friend.

In telling the story of the Freedom Vote, though, I didn't want to rehash the existing narrative, one told expertly by Joseph Sinsheimer and Bill Lawson. Through the extant archival documents, and newspaper records maintained by Stanford and Yale, we have a pretty good idea of who actually traveled east and south to help organize that frenetic campaign. To my mind, these fifty to sixty undergraduates set the nation on a course that would forever change its racial history. I wanted to find them, if only to say "thank you." Holt Ruffin opened up the Stanford part of the story for me, by returning a stranger's odd Facebook Messenger query. Fowler "Skip" Martin let me in on his private stash of documents, his remarkable memory, and the inner workings of the *Stanford Daily*, where he and Ilene

Strelitz ran a fairly sophisticated media operation, one that clearly had the president of the university's attention. Frank Dubofsky, the erstwhile pulling guard on the football team, also shared memories from his few days racing across the country to help organize this quixotic political happening. He admitted that resisting the siren song of Al Lowenstein, his professor the year prior, was simply not in the cards. Dwight Clark, not the Dwight Clark of San Francisco 49ers fame, but dean-level fame at Stanford, also helped me understand the administrative dynamics at the university. The Yale side of the Freedom Vote story remains to be told in greater detail, even as the *Yale Daily News* is a terrific source of information. Frank Basler shared with me his memory of getting arrested for passing out campaign literature in Indianola, even as the Justice Department quickly arrived at the local jail to interview him. He was headed back to New Haven after only two days in state.

Of the many things the Freedom Vote accomplished, perhaps the one the Council of Federated Organizations did not see coming involved the White Knights of the Ku Klux Klan. The leader of that organization, Sam Bowers, quickly discerned what was next: a much more robust effort to enfranchise Black Mississippians. Different klaverns were directly involved in the 1964 murders of at least five men: Charles Moore and Henry Dee on May 2 and of course Andrew Goodman, James Chaney, and Mickey Schwerner on June 21. These murders put into motion the events that occupy these pages. My journey with this history began with a 2006 documentary on Freedom Summer, and it continues quite literally to the present day.

One of my external and anonymous reviewers for this project made one very urgent request, which I honor here. "I believe the text would greatly benefit by a comment from the author—perhaps in more than one place—that he acknowledges the potential implications/impacts his work may have on experiences of historical trauma and racial pain." Reviewer A, a self-identified African American, is right: reliving the gruesome details of what happened to so many young Black men (and women, and children) demands an acknowledgement that writing about Black pain, suffering, and death can and does (re)traumatize. In telling the stories of Moore, Dee, Goodman, Chaney, and Schwerner, my aim is to document the extent of the racial hatred that motivated their killings and try to contextualize just what these volunteers and COFO workers confronted on a daily basis. Documenting that sadism and cruelty can indeed be very traumatizing.

Such trauma can spill over into memory, and I spend the second half of this project detailing specific memory events and texts, the ways in which the awful events of 1964 continue to play themselves out in a culture of remembrance—and thus, a culture of forgetting, too. Even as we continue to witness Confederate memorials hoisted out of parks, city streets, campuses, and public squares, new memorials take their place; such is the dynamism inherent to who and what a culture chooses to remember, where and when. On the campus of Miami University in Oxford, Ohio, for example, three student dormitory lobbies were dedicated in 2021 to the memories of Goodman, Chaney, and Schwerner. No doubt additional memorials bearing the names of different civil rights martyrs will continue to proliferate on American landscapes in the years ahead. And literally on the day I'm sending off this project, the state of Mississippi dedicated a new memory marker to Charles Moore and Henry Dee, at the very spot in Meadville where the Klan abducted them, replacing the makeshift, vernacular marker often vandalized and destroyed.

What remains curious and rather urgent to me as a scholar of the American civil rights movement is when memory and history collide, which they do often in the telling of this story. If historians, journalists, filmmakers, and others adopt rather uncritically a preferred memory of what supposedly happened during the search for Goodman, Chaney, and Schwerner, how does this affect what constitutes history, and with what effects on its many audiences? Does it matter that an eleventh-grader in Mansfield, Ohio, tells his classmates that eight unidentified Black bodies were discovered during the search for the three missing men? Does it matter when a full professor tells that same story to her peers at a conference, or in publication? Does it matter when that same story appears on a museum wall, or in the pages of *The Atlantic*? And just where did that preferred memory originate? And why? Whose preferences are represented? Who's forgotten?

What if the memory/history isn't true? Does someone want it to be true, in spite of the evidence? Who? And, why?

These are some of my questions in this project. As a rhetorical critic, I attempt to answer them by asking this question: What persuasive work gets done with such claims? The repetition of purportedly factual information, and the proliferation, and even exaggeration, of those claims, tells me something important might be going on. My job is to figure out what it might be. In the present case, yes, I'm most interested in the number of supposedly unidentified Black bodies discovered in Mississippi in the summer of 1964, but I'm just as interested in understanding the rhetorical work performed by repeating that shocking claim.

As of this writing, in July 2021, claims of unidentified Black bodies discovered during the search for Goodman, Chaney, and Schwerner continue to proliferate.

Speaking of memory and history, just a note about the dedication page. Before she was Ingrid Houck, she was Ingrid Holzinger, and then Ingrid Hatten, who came of age in postwar Wiesbaden, Germany, where any talk of Hitler and the Third Reich was forbidden. She eventually moved to the United States and flew the flag of her new country in the front yard of every home where she lived. We traveled the country together, piecing civil rights stories together from different archives. She was a ready researcher: patient, eager, and perhaps a bit opportunistic, too. At the Mississippi Department of Archives and History in 2010, we worked on microfilm machines a few stations apart. I was delighted to hear her machine printing repeatedly, as clearly she was finding all kinds of great newspaper material for this particular project. Later, as I gathered all of her printed pages, I glanced at her trove of documents. I couldn't believe it: they were all recipes she wanted for her own kitchen archive! I miss her. We miss her.

BLACK BODIES IN THE RIVER

Some there are who have left behind them a name to be commemorated in story. Others are unremembered, they have perished as though they had never existed, as though they had never been born.

—ECCLESIASTICUS 44:8–9

They'll find some new bodies on the weekend. That's when everybody goes fishing, so some new bodies will turn up.

—JULIAN BOND, COMMUNICATIONS DIRECTOR, STUDENT NON-VIOLENT COORDINATING COMMITTEE, JULY 30, 1964

The river is just right.

—ANONYMOUS JAILER, COLUMBUS, MISSISSIPPI

Even as newspaper editors around the state raged about the "communist invaders," the "beatnik hippies," and always, it seemed, the "sex-obsessed sophomores," Mr. and Mrs. James Bowles did what many Mississippians, white and Black, liked to do on the humid, sultry summer weekends: they went fishing. Formed when the Mississippi River cut a new path, the Old River is a sluggish backwater that curves west around the ghostly and long-abandoned Davis Plantation, Brierfield, a twenty-five-thousand-acre cotton expanse, south and west of Vicksburg, once owned and operated by the president of the Confederacy and his brother.[1]

From their small skiff, and nearing noon, Mrs. Bowles noticed what appeared to be a floating log.[2] As they moved closer, the floating object revealed its secret: splayed across the log was a pair of jeans, the legs of which were bound together by hay wire. Startled by their discovery, the Bowleses knew better than to try and retrieve the ghostly jeans missing a head and torso. Quickly did they return to shore and find a pay phone; they called Clayton Cox at the Tallulah (Louisiana) Police Department and reported what they'd seen near the Palmyra Chute off the Old River. Officer Cox quickly notified fish and game officials in both Louisiana and Mississippi; Joseph Sullivan and the Federal Bureau of Investigation were also called about the grisly Sunday discovery. A huge press contingent, headquartered mostly in Meridian, Mississippi, more than 150 miles away, packed its cameras and film and sprinted west toward the Old River; this might be the break they'd been waiting twenty-one days for. Nineteen-year-old John Rogan also got a call at a funeral home in Tallulah, Louisiana; he quickly grabbed a pair of gloves and a body bag and headed for Parker's Landing. With two other men piloting the small skiff into the swollen chute, Rogan attempted to put the remains snagged on the log into the body bag. A foot fell off as he tried to gently dislodge the brittle cadaver.

By Monday morning, July 13, newspapers in nearby Natchez reported what many locals were only whispering: the body of missing civil rights worker Michael "Mickey" Schwerner might have finally been discovered. Why Schwerner? The twenty-four-year-old Congress of Racial Equality (CORE) organizer and Cornell graduate always wore jeans and sneakers; the corpse appeared to be white; and perhaps most revealing of all, the jeans were fastened by a leather belt with a letter "M" belt buckle. Surely the other two missing workers, Andrew Goodman and James Chaney, were nearby, somewhere in the murky waters of the Old River.[3]

More law enforcement and FBI officials quickly and expertly moved in with grappling hooks and seines. Additional local, regional, and national press also quickly assembled. A second headless body, also bound at the hands and feet with hay wire, was discovered on Monday. Navy frogmen from Charleston, South Carolina, were ordered in to determine if, in fact, the Old River was a Klan boneyard. The grotesque discoveries even had the ear of President Lyndon Johnson, who was informed on July 13 by FBI director J. Edgar Hoover that bodies had been recovered.[4]

But whoever drowned the two bodies had made one critical error: In their haste to dispose of the bodies, in their attempts to forever sink the evidence of their crimes and the identities of their victims, they hadn't searched both bodies' pockets for identifying clues. On the first body was a jeans pocket and a wallet, a selective service card, and a key bearing the inscription VD1–47. The second body pulled from the Old River also contained a selective service card in a back pocket.

In this wholly accidental manner did officials identify the two headless and badly decomposed corpses as Charles Eddie Moore and Henry Hezekiah Dee. Both Black. Both only nineteen years old. Neither involved with civil rights. Both were locals who'd gone missing on May 2 from their homes in Franklin County, in the Ku Klux Klan hotbed of southwestern Mississippi. And both, according to the white Mississippi press, were "good negroes." In other words, Moore and Dee were quiet, humble, and hardworking.[5] They were certainly not part of the invading communists out to change Mississippi's "way of life." They were emphatically not Goodman-Schwerner-Chaney. As such, they were not part of the Summer Project.

Not yet.

• • •

Of course we know that the bodies of Andrew Goodman, Mickey Schwerner, and James E. Chaney ("JE") were eventually found. Buried under several tons of fill dirt on the Old Jolly Farm located just six miles south and west of Philadelphia, Mississippi, their story has largely become *the* story of the summer of 1964, what we today know as Freedom Summer. And perhaps more than any other discrete episode in the civil rights movement, the events of June, July, and August in Mississippi dominate civil rights history and civil rights memory. Julian Bond, former Student Nonviolent Coordinating Committee (SNCC) communication director, famously truncated contemporary popular civil rights history thus: "Rosa sat down, Martin stood up, and the white kids came down and saved the day."

Those "white kids," of course, were more than six hundred college students, almost exclusively white and upper middle class, purposefully recruited from elite schools such as Yale, Harvard, Oberlin, Stanford, Berkeley, Wisconsin, Queens, and Swarthmore. Recruited under the organizational umbrella of the Council of Federated Organizations (COFO)—which comprised the National Association for the Advancement of Colored People (NAACP), the Southern Christian Leadership Conference (SCLC), CORE, and SNCC—the student volunteers had a threefold mission: voter registration, the creation and operation of Freedom Schools, and creating and running local community centers.

Long before the students traveled south from their training orientation at the Western College for Women (now Miami University of Ohio) in June, though, SNCC field-workers hotly debated whether bringing such a huge influx of white students to Mississippi was strategically wise and logistically possible. Much of that debate, as I will detail, involved the issue of violence: Would the huge contingent of white men and white women provide something of a shield around the project? Wouldn't white students also bring the press, which, in turn, would at minimum interest the federal government? But even if they did, wasn't this part of the larger problem, that harming or killing a white volunteer would matter in profoundly different ways to the nation than harming or killing a native Black Mississippian? Or even "just" a Black American?

The Summer Project director, Robert Parris Moses, understood the arguments; he'd been forced to live them in ways that other SNCC'ers could not over the past three years.[6] Had he not gotten Herbert Lee, a Black father of nine, murdered in September 1961? Had he also not gotten an eyewitness to

Lee's murder, Louis Allen, murdered too? Moses, the deeply philosophical and introspective Harvard mathematician and philosopher, understood better than most how white lives and Black lives mattered very differently in the nation's racial calculus. And so the white students came.

Moses's somewhat unilateral decision, the very antithesis of SNCC's group decision-making process, was met with hostility by many on the staff. That hostility remains to this day and manifests itself rhetorically as a challenge to prevailing Freedom Summer historiography. As I will detail, some civil rights veterans—beginning as early as the late 1970s and continuing unabated in the present among activists, scholars, journalists and filmmakers—argue that many unnamed and undocumented Black bodies were discovered in Mississippi during the search for Goodman, Schwerner, and Chaney. The number of discovered Black bodies ranges anywhere from five to more than two dozen. The alarming claim that nameless Black bodies were discovered during the forty-four-day search functions rhetorically as a critique of dominant Freedom Summer history and memory, one in which Goodman, Schwerner, and Chaney are lauded as heroic martyrs while unnamed Blacks remain in the racial void, waiting to be written into the Freedom Summer narrative. How can the heroic and interracial narrative of Freedom Summer be celebrated when unnamed Black men and women were murdered in the same state, at the same time, and perhaps for the same reasons as two white college-educated men from New York—and a Black Mississippian who happened to be in their company? As I will illustrate, the historicity of the unnamed Black bodies in question is perhaps less the point than the critique of how Freedom Summer has been written, filmed, and even memorialized. The violence and death we remember and commemorate from the summer of 1964 remains largely white-on-white violence and death. Confronted by numerous deaths of nameless Black bodies and white-on-Black violence, we are invited to rethink Freedom Summer and our collective fixation on the six syllables that today form something of an American civil rights anthem: Goodman-Schwerner-Chaney.[7]

I advance my argument by dividing the project into two halves. The first half begins with the urgent fact that SNCC and its Mississippi director, Bob Moses, could not get the nation or the federal government to care publicly about Black civil rights in a state notorious for its often lethal enforcement of Jim Crow. After a brief account of SNCC's first outpost in McComb and

Liberty, I examine in detail how the 1963 Freedom Vote laid the foundation for an interracial project in which elite white college students brought with them their expertise—as well as the press and, more importantly, the federal government. The success of the Freedom Vote, though, simultaneously revived the Ku Klux Klan and white Mississippi hostility more generally, which I detail through local newspapers. I next document the Klan murders of Charles Moore and Henry Dee, as their disappearance and killing serve as the rhetorical fulcrum for what will later become the claim of unidentified Black bodies discovered during the search for Goodman, Schwerner, and Chaney, to whose murders I then turn. I close this first half of the project by noting how the deaths of Moore and Dee are rendered nameless in song and Mississippi memory, even as Goodman, Schwerner, and Chaney are rendered as Christlike movement martyrs.

The second half of this project begins with the remarkable claim—made many years after 1964 by movement veterans, academics, filmmakers, and journalists—that during the federal government's search for the three missing men, unidentified Black bodies were discovered by the FBI and law enforcement officials in Mississippi swamps, rivers, and bayous. Just how many bodies? By at least one account more than two dozen. In another instance, a number so high that it finally forced the FBI to reveal where the three men were buried in order to distract the nation's press. These claims function rhetorically at several levels, not the least of which is to question the centrality of the Goodman, Schwerner, and Chaney narrative to the larger Freedom Summer historiography. Continuing to write and celebrate their story is to continue to tell the story of white heroism—a heroism that renders unidentified Black bodies as an indictment of both historical accounts of the period as well as popular memories about it. While I examine carefully the historicity of the unnamed Black bodies claim, I also examine how different memory texts—films, landscapes, presidential speeches, and museums—function both to bolster and question the centrality of murdered white men in the larger story of Freedom Summer.

Before turning to Freedom Summer historiography and the privileged place reserved for the martyred three, we must first understand the extent to which violence generally—and expectations about interracial violence in particular—serves as a critical context for understanding how COFO's Summer Project came to be in the first place. Minus that context, which plays out over a three-year period, and which involves both the press and the federal government, Freedom Summer loses its status as a strategic and highly rhetorical response to white Mississippi's protracted campaign of violent resistance to Black equality. Without a large and interested white audience, COFO's campaign to bring civil rights to Black Mississippians would remain an unimportant story to both the national press and the federal government. How, then, to bring white America to care about Black Mississippians? And if they could be made to care, what were/are the consequences?

". . . will continue to be the Klan"

By the fall of 1963, the Student Nonviolent Coordinating Committee understood better than most civil rights organizations that violence—captured on film—had a galvanizing effect on a nation largely indifferent, if not openly hostile, to Black equality. SNCC understood this, in part, because even though the organization represented the vanguard of the student movement, it was not Martin Luther King.[8] Not a few SNCC'ers mockingly invoked "de Lawd" when talking about SCLC's eloquent leader. Whereas journalists and television cameras followed Dr. King wherever and whenever he organized, SNCC's rather lonely campaign for voting rights in Mississippi was almost unknown to the nation. Television couldn't resist the drama of water hoses and marches of Birmingham, nor the soaring eloquence at the March on Washington, but SNCCs rather undramatic work of daily organizing, voter education, and trips to the local courthouse were hardly media friendly. It didn't help that SNCC had picked the Mississippi Delta as its organizing center, either. The football-shaped alluvial plain, flooded regularly by the Mississippi River to the west, was home to some of the richest soil on earth, but its tiny media markets, uneducated populace, plantation economy, and poor accessibility hindered a national media focus.

SNCC had retreated to the Delta, and Greenwood specifically, in 1962, after effectively being flogged out of the southwestern cities of McComb (Pike County) and Liberty (Amite County) in the fall of 1961. At the behest of legendary activist Ella Baker, Bob Moses had come to Mississippi on something of a fact-finding mission for SNCC in the summer of 1960; he discovered that a few local Blacks were ready and willing to organize around the issue of voter registration. By the summer of 1961 SNCC was primed to move and eventually set up shop in McComb, at the behest of local NAACP stalwarts C. C. Bryant and E. W. Steptoe. In a state with fewer than twenty-five thousand registered Black voters, quickly did Moses and SNCC learn that even an ostensibly less confrontational approach to civil rights such as voter registration would be met with lethal white violence: "Simply attempting to register could bring on the wrath of the mob," notes Mississippi civil rights historian John Dittmer.[9] On August 22, Moses was badly beaten outside of the Amite County Courthouse, requiring eight stitches to his head. Later, on September 25, Herbert Lee, an NAACP activist and Moses's frequent driver, was executed by Mississippi state representative E. H. Hurst at a local cotton gin. While Hurst claimed self-defense and that his gun had accidently discharged, it was clear to Moses that Lee's willingness to help SNCC had gotten him killed. Louis Allen, as I will detail, was singularly unlucky to have been an eyewitness to the murder. Several weeks later, and sentenced with several colleagues to a lengthy jail term, Moses and SNCC quietly fled southwestern Mississippi in December 1961 after finally bonding out of the Pike County Jail in Magnolia. The white violence, along with ambivalent local support, had overwhelmed SNCC's first attempt to bring the franchise to Black Mississippians. Among SNCC'ers, a conclusion formed rather quickly: "nothing would happen in Mississippi, and in the South, unless somebody was willing to die."[10] The question was, who?

By the late summer of 1963, several Black Mississippians had lost their lives in the struggle for civil rights—none more prominent than the NAACP's field secretary, Medgar Evers, gunned down in his north Jackson driveway in the early morning hours of June 12. Whereas the southwestern part of the state had proven too much for SNCC's meager resources, the Delta was far more receptive to its unique approach to activism. Dominated by huge cotton plantations for more than one hundred years, the Delta was home to sizable majorities of would-be Black citizens; in some counties those majorities ran to more than 70 percent. Furthermore, World War II veterans and activists such as Amzie Moore, Dr. T. R. M. (Theodore Roosevelt Mason) Howard, and Clarksdale pharmacist Dr. Aaron Henry had cultivated important terrain—terrain very welcoming to SNCC's sensibility of nurturing local Black leadership, living in the community, and working with local youth to generate interest and eventually bring their parents into the movement. In Greenwood, SNCC organizer Sam Block helped recruit the McGhee, Greene, and Jordan families; in Sunflower County, Charles McLaurin was introduced to the remarkable Fannie Lou Hamer, a forty-four-year-old wife, mother, sharecropper, and timekeeper with a big voice and a fearless will to vote and become "a first-class citizen."

While SNCC developed local organizing talent and tried to recruit Blacks to register and vote, working within the system proved to be extremely frustrating. Why? First, white county registrars had tremendous discretion as to who they would allow to try and register, let alone pass. Not only did Mississippi have a poll tax and a literacy requirement, but beginning in 1954, would-be registrants had to be able to read and interpret, to the registrar's satisfaction, any of the more than 280 sections of the state's constitution. Second, and greatly compounding matters, Black men and women seeking to register would typically have their names and addresses printed in the local newspaper; as such, they could become a ready target for economic and/or physical reprisals. Before Fannie Lou Hamer could even return to her plantation home after registering to vote on August 31, 1962, for example, Dee Marlow, the owner of the plantation on which Hamer worked, threatened to evict her—despite cotton needing picked, records needing kept, and eighteen years of loyal service to the Marlow family.[11] And third, if the registrar or the boss man didn't intervene, there was always the local White Citizens' Council, a group of so-called better citizens formed in Indianola, Mississippi (Sunflower County), in the wake of the 1954 *Brown* Supreme Court decision, to protect the state's strict adherence to its "way of life."[12] In Mississippi this meant rigidly enforced segregation and almost no Black voters. The well-financed council movement had spread quickly across Mississippi and the Deep South, and could even count as members the state's governor, Ross Barnett, as well as the arch-segregationist from Sunflower County, US senator James O. Eastland. And while the councils claimed publicly to be against violence, such an avowal did not stop individual council members from violent retribution against local Blacks standing up for the franchise.[13]

And so as SNCC continued its campaign for voting rights in Mississippi, Bob Moses and many others had grown deeply frustrated by the late summer of 1963. Countered at every move, many Mississippi Blacks simply wouldn't risk what little they had to try and register. Those who did were often fired, intimidated, or violently assaulted, and the precious few who managed to get registered had no one to vote for given the stranglehold of white supremacy on the state's name-only two-party system. To add insult to injury, the Voter Education Project (VEP), funded by the Southern Regional Council, and which financed a large portion of SNCC's registration work in Mississippi, threatened to pull its funding as the fall turned to winter; the total number of registrants was simply too low to warrant such an expense. And of course there was little if any media coverage. Most of the movement oxygen was drawn to Washington, DC, and Dr. King's Dream, and to Birmingham's 16th Street Baptist Church, where four young Black girls had been blown up on a Sunday morning by the Alabama Klan. "The Mississippi monolith has successfully survived the Freedom Rides, James Meredith at Ole Miss and the assassination of Medgar Evers," lamented Moses. "The full resources of the state will continue to be at the disposal of local authorities to fight civil rights gains. The entire white population will continue to be the Klan."[14]

Working faithfully from within the political system, Bob Moses, COFO, and SNCC could come to only one logical conclusion: the federal government had to get involved; without a national presence in the state of Mississippi, nothing could or would change. Mississippi had sealed itself off from the rest of the country, claiming loudly to anyone who would listen that the state's Black residents could readily vote—they just weren't interested. New energy, new ideas were needed. Said Edwin King, a white SNCC activist from Vicksburg who was also the chaplain at the integrated Tougaloo College in Jackson, "We needed something new, or we needed to quit."[15] They also needed some publicity—local, state, or national. As Bob Moses later lamented, there was "utter silence . . . nobody knows, and the media doesn't care."[16] One of the main reasons that the national media simply didn't feature COFO's work in Mississippi was structural in nature. As Charles Payne notes, "The frames used to cover the civil rights movement were multiple and shifting but they were always such as to obscure the organizing process." Moses and his young charges were frustrated that the "press focused on big, dramatic events while neglecting the processes that led to them."[17] On what did the predominantly white press like to focus? "In order to play, the story had to be packaged with violence or with white involvement or with the involvement of nationally known celebrities. Where violence was present, the press could be counted on to be more attentive."[18] Even so, Moses carefully noted that the 1961 murder of Herbert Lee had generated almost no national press; lethal violence visited upon poor and rural Black Mississippians simply didn't register as important. Too, if the nation wasn't looking, white Mississippians were no doubt emboldened by the lack of media attention—and the sham attempts, if there was an attempt, to bring murderers to justice. The questions remained open for Moses: How to make the media care? How to bring the federal government into Mississippi?

"... one of the most significant events of the civil rights movement"

While the origins of events are often murky, the debate in COFO turned to a plan apparently broached first by Allard Lowenstein, a liberal white Democrat and past president of the National Student Association (NSA) who was deeply involved in campus politics around the country and had close ties to Yale and Stanford. Rather than continue to work from within the system, and after witnessing firsthand the racial terror in Mississippi, Lowenstein reached for analogy: When disenfranchised Black men and women in South Africa called for a public day of mourning, it functioned rhetorically to galvanize support across the continent. Rather than a day of mourning, though, Lowenstein wondered: What about a day of voting? "What was needed," Lowenstein's biographer recounts, "was the kind of bold action that would highlight, glaringly and dramatically, the systemic ways in which Mississippi was 'different in principle' from the rest of America, and why that difference required national attention and intervention."[19] In other words, if the federal government was ever going to involve itself in Mississippi's racial politics, bold, dramatic, and highly visible action was needed.

The plan that Lowenstein, Moses, and others eventually formulated was indeed audacious and dramatic: create a parallel gubernatorial election, with parallel candidates, a parallel platform, and parallel voting places. What better way to show the entire nation (and white Mississippians) that the state's eligible Black voters would eagerly cast ballots in large numbers when given representative candidates that they themselves had nominated and when they were freed from the specter of violence and intimidation at official polling places? While the rhetorical aims that gestured out to the nation were obvious, there were more inward—"constitutive"—ones as well.[20] That is, casting a ballot for and by Black Mississippians would be a formative act of resistance, defiance, and provocation—but one largely safe from white backlash. With their mark on a ballot, sharecroppers were transformed into citizens.

In an oral history given more than twenty years after the Freedom Vote, it is clear that Moses understood that the rhetorical power of the project had both to do with the nation taking notice, and also with disenfranchised Black Mississippians' new sense of empowerment and identity. To become a voter, to cast a ballot, was to become "legitimate"—in one's own eyes. "The concept of legitimacy—[being] qualified—I mean those were concepts that we were rubbing up against in the process of trying to register people," noted Moses. "Because what the people were saying and somehow believing in their own minds was that they were not qualified. So we had to come to grips with this notion. What does this mean? Who can legitimate people? How do a people get legitimate?"[21] Ever since 1890, when the Mississippi constitution was rewritten with the express purpose of separating Black men from the franchise, voting was understood as "white folks' business."[22] Seventy-plus years later, organizers struggled mightily to get Black Mississippians to take the registration test at the courthouse.[23] But what if the ballot came to the people? What if, instead of running the white-supremacist gauntlet at the county courthouse and in local newspapers, would-be voters cast ballots at barbershops, churches, and Black-owned businesses? Further, what if they could vote for candidates who not only looked like them but also represented their interests? The idea was a revelation to Moses: that sort of self-actualization would, in turn, release people's creative energy to get others involved. "Energy—how is [it] that you can make a move to release peoples' energy? Now those were problems that we had confronted, things we were working on which would have led us to want to do something like the Freedom Vote."[24]

But such a project faced two immediate and very practical questions: Who to run on the ballot and how to reach the stated goal of two hundred thousand legally cast ballots?[25] The first question was decided quickly and decisively: Clarksdale's Dr. Aaron Henry was nominated to run for governor at a Freedom Vote convention held in Jackson in early October. As president of COFO and a major force in the state's NAACP, Henry was one of the very few, perhaps only, Black leaders who might unite the older and more conservative faction of NAACP members with the younger and more radical cohort of SNCC activists and supporters. As a pharmacist in the north Delta community of Clarksdale, Henry was also somewhat inured to white economic intimidation.[26] The head of the Freedom Vote ticket, in other words, was fairly obvious; Henry's running mate was less so. Eventually, Bob Moses approached Rev. Edwin King about running as lieutenant governor. The white Methodist chaplain was initially reluctant given all the attention that was sure to follow—most of it negative. But the dream of an interracial ticket to lead Mississippi eventually proved decisive to the clergyman-turned-organizer, whose face and body were badly scarred and still recovering from a horrific traffic accident following his close friend Medgar Evers's death and funeral.[27]

The second question proved far more vexatious, acrimonious, and—ultimately—consequential: How to organize the entire state in less than five weeks? If the stated goal was two hundred thousand legitimate Black ballots, COFO simply didn't have the personnel or the funds to run such an ambitious campaign. Enter Allard Lowenstein, again. The thirty-four-year-old whirling dervish promised to solve COFO's problems: he could call in favors at both Yale and Stanford and quickly recruit fifty to sixty students to come to Mississippi and canvas would-be voters; and fundraisers on both campuses could quickly raise the money. The students would be white and male. SNCC, in particular, was ambivalent: on the one hand the students' mobility, dollars, and organizing acumen were desperately needed; on the other hand, the perils of shared leadership were many. How, for example, could a nineteen-year-old Black field-worker without a high school diploma and who'd never even been out of the state lead a cadre of white, mobile, and upper-middle-class college students in such a logistically complex undertaking? Furthermore, SNCC's organizing ethos was to allow local leadership to evolve organically.[28]

Complicating matters further, Lowenstein and others understood that a group of elite white young men from the nation's finest universities traveling to Mississippi to register Black voters in a parallel "mock election" would engender press coverage. This last point clearly raised some hackles among COFO regulars: white kids from west and east taking time from their busy schedules to perform a Peace Corps–like mission trip to Mississippi mattered to the nation in ways that Black field-workers who'd been organizing for more than two years simply did not. Implicit in the racial calculus, too, was the issue of violence; specifically, young, white, upwardly mobile men from prominent families could plausibly provide a very real shield during a campaign that threatened to provoke white Mississippians across the entire state. Would the local redneck, eager "to whoop some ass," be quite so enthusiastic when an out-of-state press, keen to chronicle and dramatize its best and brightest, watched? Perhaps more importantly, would local law enforcement intimidate, arrest, and brutalize when those arrested were not local Mississippi Blacks? What if the Justice Department actually showed up in Mississippi to protect the white students, and thus by default Black COFO workers? The (inter)racial crucible had almost never been turned up to such a degree in this, the Short Hot Fall.

On the other hand, what if the white volunteers did provoke violence and perhaps even murder, creating not a shield or a hesitation but a provocation? What then? And was this possibility something to be feared or embraced? Could it be both? If the white twenty-year-old student government president from Stanford University was murdered by the Klan in the racial hotbed of Franklin County, wouldn't such a high-profile killing create such outraged national and international publicity that official white Mississippi would have to capitulate? Or would this be the opening act in a protracted race war—guerilla, propaganda, or otherwise? And capitulate to whom and for what? Too, what if the white volunteers also brought their racial paternalism to Mississippi? Even as students aimed to help rural, uneducated, and extremely poor Black Mississippians get organized, the perils of an overweening white superiority were legion. Did it matter to Bob Moses and Allard Lowenstein that many Black SNCC organizers were lukewarm at best about the project?

The white college students came.

"... that boy is going to call his daddy"

The students quickly fanned out across the five congressional districts of the state, securing voting locations as well as spreading the word about the Henry/King ticket and their progressive platform featuring education, economics, and—always—desegregation.[29] The student volunteers would return north and west in early November to their cloistered campuses as conquering heroes; their student newspapers had faithfully chronicled their trials, tribulations, and triumphs.[30] Stanford junior Frank Dubofsky and sophomore Holt Ruffin were exhausted: they'd pulled out of Palo Alto early on the morning of October 27 and returned to campus six days later.[31] Along with three other Stanford undergraduates, the men drove more than two thousand miles to Jackson without stopping, except for gasoline, and did the same coming home. A starting guard on the varsity football team, Dubofsky had a bit more time on his hands in fall quarter, as he'd quit the team. Dubofsky had taken Lowenstein's class on South Africa as a freshman and, like many young men with whom Lowenstein interacted, quickly became a devotee. After the group arrived at COFO headquarters in Jackson, Bob Moses gave each man his marching orders: Holt Ruffin headed north and east to Tupelo, where he was asked to coordinate with several Black pastors to get ballot boxes into local churches. Ruffin spent nights with movement-friendly Black families, a host-guest model that would be used to great effect during Freedom Summer.

While each performed different duties around the state, the Stanford activists had two people they faithfully reported to back on campus: Fowler "Skip" Martin and Ilene Strelitz, who edited the *Stanford Daily*. Martin often served as the point of contact, answering the phone and getting important details to Strelitz, who, in turn, quickly published them in the *Daily*. The media strategy worked to great effect, as the Freedom Vote story was front-page news in Palo Alto for several weeks. Strelitz understood, too, just how race and media clout mattered to the dynamic story and Stanford's role in it: "The arrival of [white] Stanford and Yale students and support forced the national press to realize that the exposure of the written word still has a role in Mississippi. . . . It is a sad commentary upon the insensitivity of our time that the national media could be drawn in only by Northern white students and that they ignored the dedicated civil rights workers who were in the South months before Stanford students arrived, and will be there for months to come."[32] None of this would have surprised Bob Moses, who understood better than most that white college students with prestigious pedigrees gave COFO the ability and mobility to organize the state. If they, too, at long last brought the nation's media into the "closed society," he could live with the "insensitivity."

Stanford students Hugh Smith, Dennis Sweeney, Fred Goff, Ruffin, and Dubofsky weren't the only ones in contact with Strelitz and Martin at the newspaper. Lowenstein and Moses also reached out to Stanford media outlets as the Freedom Vote got underway. Strelitz, for example, could report in a Halloween Day article that the auspices for national news coverage were promising. "Moses stated that ABC, CBS, NBC, and the *New York Times* have contacted Henry headquarters. The Collegiate Press Service has released lengthy information on Stanford activities to campuses throughout the nation." The usually subdued and diffident Moses was grateful: "We can't express what Stanford support has meant." He urged students to keep the pressure on Mississippi by reaching out to their hometown newspapers as well as their representatives in Congress. While Lowenstein also kept a keen eye on the press and publicity for the Freedom Vote, his letter received at the *Daily* on the 30th also contained auspicious news: the "justice department may be moving in on Mississippi shortly."[33] Lowenstein's optimism was borne out as Burke Marshall, assistant attorney general and head of the Justice Department's Civil Rights Division, was actually on the ground in Mississippi. Moses and Lowenstein had to be pleased: the federal government's top legal official for civil rights was taking the lives of elite white college men very seriously. If that's what it also took to protect the lives of Black Mississippians, so be it.

John Herbers reported on the Freedom Vote for the *New York Times*. But it's clear from his coverage that his editors back in Atlanta—he'd been hired at the *Times* in 1963 to cover the race beat—were not eager to feature the "mock election" story coming out of Jackson. The *Times* ran just three bylined stories over the course of nine days, all relegated to the back pages of the paper. Not surprisingly, two of the three stories featured the white Yale and Stanford students, specifically the arrests of several students around the state. Nothing from Herbers's reporting, though, suggests that he was physically in the state, talking with the student volunteers, Aaron Henry, Ed King, Bob Moses, or Allard Lowenstein. Most certainly Herbers was not talking with Black Mississippians about the franchise.[34]

While the Stanford students were making telephone calls and mailing letters back to campus, and Herbers was likely making phone calls from the *Times*'s offices in Atlanta, the students from Yale University had a much more sophisticated media operation: They actually had journalists from the *Yale Daily News* in Mississippi writing bylined stories from different voter registration locations in the state. In fact, the chairman of the *Daily News*, future vice presidential candidate Joseph Lieberman, was a student volunteer. They also had three or four times the number of volunteers thanks to the celebrated Yale chaplain William Sloane Coffin, who recruited the students once Lowenstein, a 1954 Yale Law School graduate, asked for help. Assisting Coffin was law student Timothy Jenkins, who'd helped Moses and SNCC with legal matters in Mississippi that summer. The African American attorney-to-be also helped recruit in New Haven, where he downplayed the specter of serious violence: "The police are rough. You may be picked up and beaten. Still, this is very doubtful as we will be in the public spotlight."[35] A significant part of the spotlight was, in fact, Yale's journalists, who covered several corners of the state in no small detail. One of their first stories was something of a coup: getting Mississippi governor Ross Barnett to consent to an interview in Jackson. The governor dutifully stated that "Negroes are happy in Mississippi," a standard response to nearly all race-inflected queries.[36]

Two of Coffin and Jenkins's recruits, Peter Kornblum and Franklin Basler, arrived in Jackson on the morning of Tuesday, October 22. By that evening they'd been arrested by the Indianola police for distributing copies of the *Mississippi Free Press* in a local Black neighborhood. While Herbers didn't report the arrest in the *New York Times* until October 30, the *Yale Daily News* featured the story the next day, on its front page.[37] Several other COFO activists were also arrested that evening in Indianola, but the *Daily News* focused exclusively on the white sophomore and senior. In an oral history conducted more than fifty years later, Kornblum noted that just a few hours after their arrest, the two were being interviewed, in person, by lawyers from the Justice Department.[38] Given that they were two of the first Yale students to be on the ground in Mississippi, it is clear that the federal government had anticipated possible violence—and moved quickly to put local law enforcement on notice that they were being closely watched. No doubt this unprecedented attention rankled the police, several of whom had participated in savagely beating civil rights protesters—in and out of jail. While the *Daily News* featured more stories about student arrests as October closed, there was also the more quotidian reality of daily organizing: making phone calls, mimeographing, coordinating, and strategizing. "For most of these local workers," Soltman and Van Dyke reported, "no headline stories appear. Because of their work for this election, their future in Mississippi will be made as difficult as possible by the white community.

No spectacular results appear, but the drama of the battle for democracy goes on day after day."[39]

Many activists in SNCC and COFO, though, weren't enamored of the white volunteers' mad dash through Mississippi. SNCC executive secretary Jim Forman chafed in particular at one Lowenstein protégé who insisted that he be allowed to canvas in the dangerous area of Yazoo City, COFO directives and warnings be damned: "If Lowenstein told him to go to heaven and Moses said he should go to hell, then he'd better start packing his summer clothes."[40] The student volunteer ended up being expelled by the city's police almost before he could cross the county line.[41] Others resented how the white press had seemingly fawned over the privileged white elite and their Pied Piper, Lowenstein. And then there was editorializing about the supposedly backward and morally deficient "Mississippi Negro" from Yale's in-state reporter, Jon Van Dyke: "What is vitally needed is for self-respect and determination to be instilled into the Negro. He must be taught that there are steps to be taken, and that the advantages that he can gain from voting are greater than the risks required by registrations." After just two days in state, Van Dyke could conclude that "the white community will most certainly not respect the Negro until the Negro can respect himself. And this will not come about until the Negro realizes the value of the civil rights movement and agrees to fight to change the Mississippi status quo. One way to speed this process is for educated white Northerners to come to Mississippi and help the Negro understand democracy."[42] Such thinly veiled white savior/supremacy rhetoric had to anger the activists who had suffered for more than two long years trying to enact the very democracy that Van Dyke and others imperiously extolled. COFO did not need Yalies or anybody else telling them how to do their supremely difficult and perilous jobs.

They might have also chafed, or just broken out into hives, if they read the *Daily News* story from November 11. Veterans of the campaign assembled on campus at the Stiles Lounge to quite literally sip sherry, congratulate one another, and celebrate their collective and individual heroism. "There was an air of victory surrounding the gathering of Mississippi returnees Friday afternoon," Van Dyke opened. "As each student walked into the Ezra Stiles lounge, he quietly poured himself a glass of sherry . . . and began exchanging stories. . . . they all laughed at the successive examples of police harassment."[43] Bob Moses arrived late to the sherry sipping. His mind was still on how news of the Freedom Vote was circulating: "We made a breakthrough toward the end of the campaign, a breakthrough in the press and [we] were well covered by the AP and UPI. We also got time on TV and could explain our position to whites and Negroes."[44] Van Dyke did not report on what Moses was drinking.

Part of the genius of the Freedom Vote strategy was to remove the threat of white intimidation and violence by having voters cast ballots in safe places: neighborhoods, barbershops and beauty parlors, and always local Black churches. Additionally, in securing names, ages, and addresses to determine eligibility to vote in this parallel election, COFO was simultaneously creating an enormous statewide inventory of Black men and women willing to stand up and be counted; it remained to be seen if and how that inventory might eventually be leveraged.

As field organizers and their college charges organized across the state, COFO also continued its innovative approach to "incidents" that happened along the campaign trail: arrests, violence, threats. Basically any event that interrupted the workers' mission was recorded in detail—and the more specific the better. Perhaps not surprisingly, the "events" came rolling into state headquarters in Jackson: Yale graduate student Bruce Payne and SNCC field-worker George Greene were pummeled in broad daylight after stopping to buy gasoline at a station in the Mississippi River town of Port Gibson; two nights later Greene and Payne barely escaped a harrowing encounter with the Natchez Klan, limping to safety on a bullet-riddled back tire. One of the men eventually arrested for the intimidation and beating was Klansman Myron Wayne "Jack" Seale, whose surname would resurface in the spring and summer of 1964. The daily and detailed archive of events chronicled by COFO, of course, was no mere descriptive list or catalogue of daily arcana, however violent; rather, it functioned rhetorically as a persuasive dossier of Mississippi's organized resistance to voting rights—a dossier easily leveraged with a press corps keen to write about this cross-racial and cross-national campaign. White Mississippi resistance, in other words, was not anecdotal but systemic and organized.

Completed Freedom Vote ballots grew exponentially as the Monday, November 4, deadline came and went. Large numbers of votes were cast in the north Delta and in and around Jackson. That night, at the Jackson Masonic Temple celebration, Bob Moses, Allard Lowenstein, Ed King, and

Aaron Henry exuberantly, if somewhat deliriously, declared victory.[45] No, the Henry/King ticket did not threaten to unseat Paul Johnson, who'd won the Democratic primary back in August, and thus the general election.[46] The victory was thoroughly rhetorical: with tens of thousands of Freedom Ballots cast, Black Mississippians had eagerly demonstrated that they wanted to vote; when free from intimidation they voted in mass; the fifty to sixty white volunteers had not been maimed or killed in the process; and the press had given some attention to this admittedly curious exercise in protest politics.[47]

As COFO no doubt anticipated, the press's attention was largely indifferent to Black COFO organizers and the Black Mississippi men and women exercising the (parallel) franchise for the first time. As Dittmer notes, "The media's fixation on the white students remained constant until the end of the campaign."[48] Lowenstein and SNCC organizer Mendy Samstein observed that the television cameras during the November 4 celebration in Jackson were pointed in just one direction: "The TV cameras were all there (and) they focused again on . . . the white students. And the bitterness of the SNCC workers was very understandable and intense."[49] James P. Marshall, who worked at the *Yale Daily News*, notes that "where the Mississippi African American had been passed over as not being newsworthy, this was not the case with white middle-class students."[50] Furthermore, "white students being beaten and shot at by southern racists was not the same as African American civil rights workers and local African Americans being put in jail, murdered, and generally harassed and intimidated." Typical of the national press's interest in the Freedom Vote was this lede from John Herbers of the *New York Times*: "About 50 Yale University students have been in Mississippi for the last 10 days working in behalf of a Negro candidate for Governor. Several have been arrested."[51] Those several were later identified by name in the *Times's* story. Little wonder, then, that Black COFO and SNCC workers, many of whom had worked for two years in the state and faced daily violence, "reacted bitterly" to the media's neglect.[52]

The final vote tally was indeed impressive: nearly eighty thousand votes cast in a campaign that lasted less than three weeks, done on a shoestring budget with outsiders who knew little about the state's geography or its racial politics. Auspicious, too. Not long after the campaign, Dave Dennis, a CORE field-worker and COFO higher-up, wrote up a postmortem on the quixotic event. Even though some deemed the Freedom Vote "silly" or a "plaything," its results were nothing short of a revelation: "it did much more for the movement toward uniting Mississippi than anything else we have done." Moreover, since Black Mississippians had never before been organized to this extent, "we just cannot afford to let it go back."[53]

A different revelation was observed by several in SNCC, including the Trinidadian-born Howard University student Stokely Carmichael. The future chairman of SNCC remarked in his memoir, "The thing that was most instructive, though, was the violence. During the three weeks the volunteers from elite private universities were in the state, nobody—local person or volunteer—was badly hurt." Despite the fact that the Freedom Vote was "the most visible, active, far-reaching, and provocative political activity SNCC had yet attempted, the level of violence had not noticeably risen. In fact, [it] had seemed to diminish? Odd."[54] Regarding Carmichael's last point, Moses explained it to him thus: "That was the first time that I realized that the violence could actually be controlled. . . . That it wasn't totally random. I realized that somewhere along the line, there was someone who, even if they didn't actually order it to happen, could at least send out word for it to stop." That the heretofore random and lethal white-on-Black/white violence could be predicted, tempered, and perhaps even shut off "was a revelation" to the man whose head had been bludgeoned in Liberty and whose bold vision had put a husband and father of nine in the grave.[55] The differences—in fact the only notable difference—between the summer campaign in Pike, Amite, and Walthall Counties and the fall Freedom Vote two years later involved the scale and participation of the white college students. To a mathematician and keen logician like Bob Moses, that one variable seemed to provide overwhelmingly conclusive proof that only an interracial calculus could crack open the state to federal intervention. But just how big did that variable need to be? Fifty to sixty white male students from Stanford and Yale, give or take, working on something not quite "real," with no legal standing, and in the relative safety of Black neighborhoods, churches, and communities was one thing. To do it for keeps, for real, and with actionable mandates, at the courthouse, in all corners of the state—that was a qualitatively and quantitatively different thing.

The judgement of Carmichael and Moses about the comparative lack of violence encountered during the three-week Freedom Vote campaign stands in notable contrast to a number of more-recent historical accounts detailing the mock election.[56] Chafe, for example, claims that "the state of

Mississippi responded with hysteria toward both the Freedom Vote and the white students.... Each day new episodes of violence and intimidation were reported, some of them coming perilously close to murder."[57] Dittmer argues that "police harassed and jailed campaign workers throughout the state" and that "life-threatening confrontations" were often part of the more than two hundred recorded arrests.[58] Similarly, Hogan details how whites responded in "traditional fashion" to the voting campaign, as well as "the terror inflicted on civil rights workers in Mississippi."[59] And Sinsheimer describes how Mississippi "state officials responded with traditional forms of harassment. Student volunteers were shot at, beaten, jailed, and arrested on a variety of curfew and traffic violations."[60]

Like his SNCC colleagues Moses and Carmichael, however, Lawrence Guyot noted the very different atmosphere of the Freedom Vote. Sure, there were arrests and countless threats, but the mock election would have no martyrs, Black or white. For Guyot, the relative lack of violence wasn't just because the white students and the white press were in Mississippi. No, the bigger fact, the more consequential difference, was that the FBI and the Justice Department were also in the state: "Wherever those white volunteers went, FBI agents followed. It was really a problem to count the number of FBI agents who were there to protect the students. It was just that gross."[61] That "gross"-ness angered many Black workers in COFO, who resented the attention that white students attracted from the federal government.[62] But Greenwood native George Greene, whose entire family was active in the movement, was not resentful of the radical shift occasioned by white students like Yale's Bruce Payne riding shotgun with him: "See if you want to shoot me you were going to have to shoot a white boy too. And I don't think you can get away with shooting that white boy cause his daddy is a Congressman in the United States Congress." The fearless SNCC organizer who defied the Klan in the very dangerous southwestern part of the state continued, "If you shoot me, if you do anything to me, the world will know about it because I know that that boy is going to call his Daddy each and every night and tell him what happened. I am going to say my blessings with him because he is keeping me alive. He is keeping me alive."[63]

In a word, elite white undergraduates from Yale and Stanford and their collective well-being mattered intrinsically to the federal government, but the students also had a hand in shaping the government's newfound interest in Mississippi. COFO's rhetorical strategy going into the Freedom Vote was to leverage the students' access to levers of federal power. On October 28, for example, Yale student Kenneth Klotz wrote a lengthy letter to his Indiana senator, Birch Bayh, describing the anarchy in the state: "My experiences here in two days of field work have bordered on the unbelievable." After detailing several instances of police harassment and intimidation, Klotz also noted the standard refutation offered by white Mississippians: "I have been told that I am an outside agitator, meddling in the affairs of others because I am from Indiana and not from Mississippi. Senator Bayh, as a human being and as a citizen of the United States of America, this *is* my business." White Mississippi's standard response to civil rights organizing was something of a tu quoque argument: look in your own backyard before you come to ours. Klotz, though, strategically locates white racism not in the community but in law enforcement's willingness to interfere with voting rights; as such, the federal government might take an active interest in such an abuse of state power. "I beg you to work with all your fervor and influence," Klotz closed, "to alleviate this shameful perversion of law and order."[64]

COFO, of course, also released the Klotz letter to the press. Other students sent letters to their hometown newspapers documenting the different world of Mississippi. COFO also kept up a steady stream of requests for federal protection. One telegram to President Kennedy began, "DEMAND IMMEDIATE DISPATCH OF FEDERAL MARSHALS TO PROTECT CAMPAIGN WORKERS FROM GROWING HARASSMENT THROUGHOUT MISSISSIPPI. OVER 200 INCIDENTS INVOLVING POLICE VIOLATION OF CONSTITUTIONAL RIGHTS HAVE OCCURRED IN LAST TEN DAYS."[65] While Kennedy never responded directly to their request, it's clear that the Kennedy Justice Department was listening; after all, COFO's careful documentation alleged violations of the Fifteenth Amendment. A federal presence in the form of marshals was not sent to Mississippi; Oxford, James Meredith, and the smoldering stench of tear gas were still too fresh in the nostrils of the executive branch. But the more subdued approach of dark suits, ties, and notebooks had Lawrence Guyot's attention. White Mississippians', too.

By all accounts the Freedom Vote was a stunning, and largely unexpected, success. Though the program didn't hit its audacious goal of two hundred thousand ballots, nearly eighty thousand Black Mississippians cast their votes for progressive policies and an interracial ticket; the energy and legitimacy that Moses hoped would be released was; the press covered the campaign, even as the *Stanford Daily* and the *Yale Daily News* made it a sensational three-week event; the FBI and the Justice Department finally came to Mississippi; nobody was badly hurt; student fundraising on both campuses paid for bail and many campaign expenses; and the entire state was finally organized for future political action. Dave Dennis, Stokely Carmichael, Bob Moses, George Greene, and Lawrence Guyot all sensed that in four short weeks something foundational had shifted. Freedom Rider, 1963 SNCC chairman, and future congressman John Lewis sensed it as well. Before the vote had even concluded, he announced that the "freedom ballot . . . is one of the most significant events of the civil rights movement."[66] This from one of the "Big Six" civil rights leaders, who'd only recently been a headliner at the March on Washington. And all because a few dozen white college kids from Palo Alto and New Haven had taken quick breaks during their academic terms to travel to Mississippi and help. As COFO and SNCC activists headed to the relatively progressive Mississippi River city of Greenville in mid-November to reflect on what they'd learned during the Freedom Vote, and what might come next, a critical threshold had been breached, one from which there would be no turning back. As Mills notes, without hyperbole, the issues raised at the meeting by thirty-five Black and seven white activists—and hotly debated over the next two months—"would dominate the civil rights movement for the remainder of the decade."[67]

"Bring a thousand whites and the country is going to react . . ."

Perhaps not surprisingly following the tectonic shift of the Freedom Vote, the critical issue raised at Greenville, and later at conferences in Jackson, Atlanta, and finally Hattiesburg, was race. More specifically, Moses raised the possibility of bringing upwards of five thousand white college students to Mississippi in 1964, a massive escalation of the Freedom Vote experiment. Why so many, so fast? Moses argued that the Citizens' Councils, the repressive state government, and the increasing mechanization of plantation life were driving Blacks out of the state; in just a few more years Mississippi Blacks might lose some of their numerical superiority, especially in the Delta. Beyond this, the uncharacteristically confrontational Moses threatened to leave SNCC altogether if the staff voted to exclude whites on a future project. Couldn't others see that whites created national publicity for their work, and that such publicity could be leveraged for, and measured in, their bodily protection? Lawrence Guyot could. So could Fannie Lou Hamer, who'd been horribly brutalized by white police officers in a Winona, Mississippi, jail in June 1963: "If we're going to break down this barrier of segregation," the former sharecropper declared, "we can't segregate ourselves."[68] Moses, Guyot, and Hamer, though, were in a decided minority at Greenville; the majority of SNCC staffers had serious reservations over a Freedom Vote on steroids. As Meier and Rudwick note, "Many COFO people resented the fact that violence against white activists was more likely to bring publicity and federal intervention than was intimidation of Blacks, and feared that articulate and well-educated white college students might usurp leadership roles."[69] The proposed Summer Project was not voted on.[70]

By late January, COFO, and SNCC more specifically, were inching closer to a scaled-down Summer Project. No doubt some of that support was because Moses continued to lobby for it. But there was also even more evidence that white outsiders could train the nation's eye on—and thus bring protection to—the state. On Monday, January 22, a delegation of fifty white clergy sponsored by the National Council of Churches and its newly formed Commission on Religion and Race, led by Robert Spike, came to Hattiesburg to participate in the state's first Freedom Day, "an unprecedented event in movement history."[71] Pioneered largely by SNCC executive director Jim Forman, who first experimented with the concept on October 7, 1963, in Selma, Alabama,[72] local Blacks assembled in the morning at the Forrest County Courthouse—named after Klan founder Nathan Bedford Forrest—and formed a long queue. Others, including many COFO staff and the observing clergy, marched in solidarity while would-be registrants waited their turn in the pouring rain. Nobody was beaten, and only one person, Bob Moses, was arrested. No doubt, Dittmer concluded, "the presence of network television cameras affected police behavior, as did the large delegation of visiting [white] clergy."[73]

Two days later, at a staff meeting in Hattiesburg, several spoke up in favor of the proposed Summer Project: Casey Hayden noted the increased attention that would ensue from both Congress and the press; Gwen Gillon offered a similar assessment; and Oscar Chase from Yale Law School also observed that "out of state people bring protection." Perhaps most persuasively, Ella Baker offered her two cents—which among SNCC staffers was a most-esteemed currency. If SNCC could be said to have a matriarch, it was Baker, the sixty-year-old Black Virginian who had organized the conference out of which SNCC was eventually created in 1960, following the student sit-ins. A formidable if often diffident presence, Baker listened more than she spoke.[74] But in Hattiesburg, she, too, noted that a sizable contingent of white students would offer COFO "leverage" in its Summer Project ambitions. And just what were those ambitions? Unlike the free-wheeling Freedom Vote, volunteers would be staffed in one of four very specific projects: voter registration, Freedom Schools, community centers, and research. Moses also envisioned a large contingent of lawyers, medical personnel, and clergy in bringing the nation to Mississippi.

Some in Hattiesburg were less optimistic; a few were downright angry. Dona Richard Moses, Bob Moses's wife, continued to be outspoken in her opposition: publicity should not be the main motive driving the project. For an organization that professed to be radically democratic, an organization that loathed the status-driven hierarchy so prevalent in other civil rights organizations, wasn't this Moses-led project anathema to SNCC's identity, even its organizing ethos of local participation? Several SNCC'ers were angered by what they perceived to be an undemocratic process.[75]

Any doubts, public or private, that Bob Moses may have had about the Summer Project ended in the evening hours of January 31. At approximately 8:30, just outside of the small southwestern Mississippi town of Liberty in Amite County, Louis Allen, a forty-four-year-old logger, NAACP member, and witness to the Herbert Lee murder, was murdered at the entrance to his property. Two shotgun blasts to the head mortally wounded the Black World War II veteran who'd asked SNCC (and the Justice Department) repeatedly for protection in light of his willingness to testify to Lee's 1961 murder at the hands of Mississippi representative E. H. Hurst. Amite County sheriff Daniel Jones, who'd broken Allen's jaw the year prior and who'd harassed him relentlessly, led the "investigation" into Allen's murder. Needless to say the case was never prosecuted.[76] After Moses learned these details firsthand from Allen's widow, the case for the Summer Project was decisive in his mind: "They [COFO] were in a position to force some national attention onto Mississippi, thereby putting pressure on the federal government to protect Black life in the state."[77] According to Moses, "There had to be a response, a larger response than we had been able to provide two years before, or would be able to provide with the people we had working now. I spoke up for the summer project, threw all my weight behind it."[78] With Allen's murder, tied directly to his initial organizing work in 1961, Moses once again had someone else's blood on his hands—and it was blood that very few whites inside or outside of Mississippi cared to acknowledge, let alone investigate and prosecute. The possibility of murdered white college students could change all that; as such, the murder of Louis Allen conclusively decided it for Moses. It was an admittedly odd trade-off—leverage white racism for progressive civil rights gains—but Bob Moses had experienced two solid years of federal hostility and indifference to the arrests, intimidation, violence, and murder. If white college kids died, so be it; he was willing to die alongside them. If they didn't, even better.

Dave Dennis agreed with Moses. In a 1977 oral history, the CORE leader and future second-in-command during the Summer Project described the racial logic: "We knew that if we had brought in a thousand Blacks, the country would have watched them slaughtered without doing anything about it. Bring a thousand whites and the country is going to react to that in two ways. First of all is to protect. We made sure that we had the children, sons and daughters, of some very powerful people in this country over there." Well-connected, upwardly mobile white students would have—and hold—the nation's attention; they might also, per the experience of the Freedom Vote, provide something of a shield. Dennis continued: The nation "would respond to a thousand young white college students, and white college females who were down there . . . and if there were gonna take some deaths to do it, the death of a white college student would bring on more attention to what was going on than for a Black college student getting it. That's cold, but that was also in another sense speaking the language of this country."[79] Of course, speaking with more than a decade of hindsight, Dennis could readily offer such a prophetic warning, but COFO's experiences in Mississippi didn't require a soothsayer's divinations: ten years after the *Brown* decision, Black lives in Mississippi were strictly a local matter—if they mattered at all. As Mills notes, COFO and SNCC were "building a vital part of the Summer Project around the belief that the same whites who could be indifferent to more Black deaths in white Mississippi would be touched if *white* students were killed."[80] Similarly, Payne argues, "[the Summer Project] was self-consciously an attempt to use the nation's racism, its tendency to react only when white life was endangered, as a point of leverage."[81]

"It still rests very heavy . . ."

COFO formally announced plans for the Summer Project, what it had dubbed Freedom Summer, on March 15, in Jackson. Claude Sitton, who reported on civil rights for the *New York Times*, announced in his lede the dramatic news: "The most extensive program of Negro education and political action seen in the South was outlined for Mississippi today by civil rights organizations."[82] While Moses would serve as the project leader, Dave Dennis of New Orleans and of the Congress of Racial Equality would serve as the associate director. With successful projects already running in Meridian (Lauderdale County) and Canton (Madison County), CORE had made major inroads in some difficult areas, especially in Canton, where businessman C. O. Chinn and Annie Devine led locals in a county whose population was 72 percent Black. At the Meridian project, led by Matt Suarez, two transplanted New Yorkers were making progress organizing local Blacks. Michael "Mickey" Schwerner and his wife, Rita, had arrived in Mississippi in January, the day before the Freedom Day event in Hattiesburg, to run a local community center. The gregarious Mickey quickly fell in with local youth, including twenty-year-old James Chaney ("JE"), who seemed to know every dirt road, every dusty hollow in Meridian, including the recently organized Klan stronghold in Neshoba County, thirty-five miles to the north and west. While Meridian had a reputation in COFO as a relatively "tension-free" area in the Fourth Congressional District, danger loomed in the more rural and clannish outlying areas. Rita quickly figured out how to get the adults involved by holding sewing classes, with all the cloth donated from up north. The Schwerners' organizing work was such that by spring, Dave Dennis informed national CORE headquarters that Mickey would direct projects in six counties during the upcoming Summer Project; moreover, Dennis noted that Freedom Schools were planned to be held in Meridian, Clarke, and Neshoba Counties. The CORE Mississippi director also recommended that James Chaney be moved up to paid staff immediately.[83]

On May 31, four days after writing his letter to CORE's national leaders, Dennis, Chaney, and Mickey Schwerner traveled to the predominantly Black Longdale community in northeastern Neshoba County; they were there to try and finalize an agreement with Mt. Zion Methodist Church officials to host a Freedom School at the rural location. Schwerner and JE were confident that Mt. Zion would agree to host the school; after all, they'd made more than thirty visits to the community in less than four months and had established loyal contacts willing to advance COFO's mission. "After conversations with Longdale's leaders, they picked out Mt. Zion Church as an ideal spot." Why? According to Carol V. R. George, "The men saw the advantage of its rural location and also its connection to a network of rural Black churches. Mt. Zion would be a place from which they could recruit other Black Methodists in the area willing to take risks to register to vote."[84] The Memorial Day meeting proved to be a success, as "the great majority of Mt. Zion's members" agreed to their request.[85] That decision would forever alter the trajectory of Freedom Summer.

It was no secret to movement organizers that the Ku Klux Klan was active once again across the state; as Klan historian Don Whitehead notes, COFO's organizing successes in Mississippi coaxed the moribund organization back into activity in 1963.[86] Driving much of that activity was Laurel businessman Sam Bowers, who'd led a move away from the Original Knights of Louisiana Klan in mid-December to form the Mississippi White Knights (MWK) of the KKK. Bowers, a college-educated veteran, proselytized with the message that "the civil rights movement was a 'Jewish-communist conspiracy' operating from Washington to win control of the United States."[87] Unlike other Klansmen, Bowers advocated for a much more aggressive organization, one in which cross burnings were not a climax but a prolegomena; "elimination"—murder, or a "number 4"— would be carried out only at his directive as imperial wizard. Well before COFO's official announcement for the Summer Project, Bowers moved quickly to assemble and orchestrate the White Knights. As spring began, a well-organized klavern of the MWK near Neshoba County announced its presence loudly: on April 4, twelve crosses burned simultaneously across the county, including on the courthouse square in downtown Philadelphia. Bowers's message had resonated deeply with a sawyer and Baptist preacher who lived near Union, Mississippi, Edgar Ray Killen, who as kleagle had done most of the recruiting for both the Lauderdale and Neshoba Klaverns.

If COFO didn't get word of the Neshoba Klan cross burnings, it couldn't have missed the shot across the bow less than three weeks later. In a massive rhetorical display of organized hostility, the White Knights simultaneously burned crosses in sixty-four of Mississippi's eighty-two counties on April 24. Such statewide organization, Bowers and the White Knights not so subtly announced, would challenge COFO's organization and aims at every point. Moreover, with the Klan actively recruiting—successfully—from within the state's law enforcement circles, civil rights workers were on their own. White student volunteers entering the state would learn quickly that the sheriffs, police, and highway patrolmen could form a Gordian knot of unapologetic—and lethal—white supremacy.[88]

Two days earlier, on Wednesday, April 22, a much less dramatic and very different "police action" had taken place at Alcorn A&M College in Lorman, less than an hour north of Natchez. SNCC did not have an active presence at Alcorn, since it was a state institution and therefore subject to the fiscal whims of the all-white Mississippi legislature, but it did take note of a curious item coming from campus: college president J. D. Boyd had suddenly suspended nearly one thousand students "for conduct on the campus unbecoming a student." The specific reason for the suspension was not included by Boyd in the brief letter mailed to students and parents, but it was apparently not a "civil rights" issue.[89] One of the students immediately suspended was freshman, Charles Eddie Moore. Nicknamed "Nub" for his physical stature, Moore had excelled academically and athletically in high school at nearby Meadville in Franklin County; Moore had also been elected president of his freshman, sophomore, and senior classes.

Two days after Alcorn had suspended a large proportion of its student body, Bob Moses was speaking to a packed house of Stanford students at Cubberley Auditorium. No doubt several of the Freedom Vote volunteers were in attendance to hear the charismatic director of the Summer Project give his recruitment pitch. In a voice barely above a whisper, the pitch turned into an existential meditation on violence, responsibility, and citizenship. In a word, it was vintage Bob Moses. The Freedom Vote had finally brought the country and the federal government to Mississippi, and while it had created its own "real, very tough problems," opening up the state was now possible. While his speech was ostensibly meant to recruit volunteers, Moses kept returning to the theme of violence, even referencing SNCC members who were "violently opposed" to the Summer Project.

And while there was "no violent white reaction" at the Freedom Day event in Hattiesburg, Moses closed the address with a searing personal account of Herbert Lee's 1961 execution. "If we hadn't gone in there," Herbert Lee "wouldn't have been killed." The unstated premise was that some—how many?—would-be summer volunteers would very likely be murdered. Innocent blood would again be shed because of his decisions; the Klan was already burning crosses. And so Moses ended his speech with a question—addressed perhaps more to himself than his audience members: "What does it mean to be involved in that kind of action, which might precipitate that kind of death?" While he, too, exposed himself to the threat of violent death, the question still "rests very heavy": the volunteers "who go down to Mississippi this summer, nobody really knows what might happen."[90] After an awkward pause, the audience rose as one and applauded. Stanford students had exactly six remaining days to get their applications in.

At Queens College in New York City, Aaron Henry's speech to the student body piqued the interest of a sophomore anthropology major, Andrew Goodman.[91] "Friends of SNCC" chapters on campuses at Berkeley and Madison set up screening interviews for prospective volunteers. With summer looming, the massive push to recruit nearly one thousand students, all of whom needed very careful vetting, stretched COFO to its limits. The aim was to have the cadre of students trained at two weeklong sessions on the campus of Berea College during the third and fourth weeks of June; the site, as well as some funding for the arriving students, had been secured by one of COFO's close allies, the National Council of Churches, and its Commission on Race and Religion.

COFO did not attempt to actively recruit volunteers from the nation's historically Black colleges and universities. The reasoning was twofold: First, students would have to provide their own bail money should they be arrested, a circumstance that greatly limited white and Black students who were cash-strapped. Perhaps more alarming for the intrepid students, COFO warned, "Believe it or not, at the moment we are absolutely broke. Our workers go without eating and our bills are piling up."[92] Second, COFO wanted the national attention, media interest, and therefore protection that only white college students from the most elite universities would engender. To quell any remaining doubts as to motive, COFO officials made plain the logic of the Summer Project in its "Prospectus for Mississippi Freedom Summer": "Previous projects have gotten no national publicity on the crucial issue of voting rights, and, hence, have little national support either from public opinion or from the federal government." Furthermore, a "large number of students from the North making the necessary sacrifices to go South would make abundantly clear to the government and the public that this is not a situation which can be ignored any longer."[93] COFO did not need to specify that the "large number of students" simply had to be white. Perhaps more troublingly, the prospectus left vague what those "necessary sacrifices" might be.

"... plans riots in Mississippi this summer"

As recruitment was carried out on campuses across the nation, COFO leaders continued a major lobbying campaign aimed directly at the White House. That campaign had one objective: federal protection of the student volunteers—both rhetorical and material; that is, COFO repeatedly implored the Johnson administration for public promises of protection, as well as the protection offered by federal marshals. By the close of April and the beginning of May 1964, enough material had been published in Mississippi newspapers for COFO leaders to understand that the rhetorical stakes had been joined. In a lengthy open letter addressed to "Friends," and authored by "Summer Project Staff," the second sentence intoned, "We have learned that this project is causing fear and hostility in the white community, because it has been characterized as an 'invasion' of several thousand college students intent upon 'agitating' and causing 'violence.'" Such a rhetorical characterization, though, "is based upon a misunderstanding of the program, and that an explanation of the project's intent and scope is needed to allay the fears of white people in Mississippi."[94] Whether the letter writers were being disingenuous or not, suffice it to say that the rhetorical toothpaste was well out of the tube: White Mississippians were not going to countenance a rhetorical "do-over" by COFO, or anyone else for that matter. No, the pending communist-inspired invasion of their state by "beatnik" white college kids arrogantly looking to change the state's way of life during two months of summer break was not a "misunderstanding" in need of more explanation.

The hostility coming out of Mississippi was unmistakable—to say nothing of the militarization of local police departments. In Jackson, for example, Mayor Allen Thompson pumped an additional $2 million (nearly $17 million in 2021) into his law enforcement budget. Other county sheriffs simply deputized more white citizens. Despite the onslaught of letters to the White House, President Johnson continued to give the cold shoulder to COFO's requests for promises of protection. Aaron Henry, Bob Moses, and Dave Dennis, the COFO triumvir, reached out to such civil rights heavies as Roy Wilkins, James Farmer, and Martin Luther King: Would they please lobby the president on behalf of the impending Summer Project?[95] COFO also decided to leverage another important constituency in its lobbying campaign: parents of the volunteers. The decision to enlist parents was both legal and strategic: legal in that parents had to give permission to allow many underage children to go to Mississippi, and strategic because of their economic, social, and political influence. In a letter dated April 27, Philadelphia, Pennsylvania, parents and relatives drafted a letter to President Johnson in which they expressed grave concern "that injury and abuse may befall our loved ones as a result of repressive measures that will be adopted by the local authorities in the south." Johnson and his administration could and should "act as an immediate and effective interface or buffer to prevent violence and harm."[96] Johnson and his subordinates chose not to reply.

The carefully orchestrated campaign to try to protect the summer volunteers can be productively interpreted as a telling barometer of concern; that is, perhaps COFO had realized in the late spring that it had overplayed its hand. Was the "on-off violence switch" experienced during the Freedom Vote simply a misleading characterization of the brief and relatively small-scale project? After all, the Kennedy Justice Department had to protect a small handful of students over the course of just a few weeks. The reaction of many white Mississippians to the pending "invasion" was literally a call to arms—white, brown, or any other color. Sam Bowers and his White Knights of the Mississippi Klan's understanding of the coming confrontation was not extremist-inspired hyperbole yelled loudly by a shrouded and shrill fringe; the likelihood of a looming race war was not premised on the ambiguities of a metaphor. Klansmen were not known for their interpretive dexterity with figures of speech. And so COFO's lobbying for federal protection continued as April turned to May, as talk of the "invasion" reached a fever pitch in Mississippi, and as the "army" of white nonviolent volunteers coalesced on the nation's most elite campuses.

In the often violent southwestern part of the state, Mississippi attorney general Joe Patterson did nothing to staunch the heated rumors about the pending summer invasion. Speaking to fifty members of the Meadville Civitan, the state's most senior elected law enforcement official claimed that "the Student Non-Violent Co-ordinating Committee plans riots in Mississippi this summer to such an extent that they hope the federal government will take over."[97] For the white businessmen of Meadville, including the owner-publisher-editor of the *Franklin Advocate* newspaper, Dave Webb, Patterson's warning hit the dreaded rhetorical trip wire that still panicked and angered many white patriotic Mississippians: the "first" Reconstruction. Webb eagerly published the attorney general's grossly misleading prediction in his newspaper; after all, as an official in the Americans for the Preservation of the White Race (APWR), a rumored Klan affiliate, Webb reveled in the coming confrontation with the communist "mixers." No doubt the White Knights klavern in Meadville, known locally as the Bunkley Klavern, read Webb's paper and Patterson's warning with interest.[98] Several weeks following the address to the Civitans, dynamite destroyed the front of the Blue Flame Café in the nearby community of Bude, just east of Meadville. Local proprietors John and Lillie V. Clark were reported to have no enemies, "white or negro."[99] Perhaps Bunkley Klansmen had heard rumors of the Clarks' friendliness to civil rights workers in need of lunch. Perhaps the Clarks simply had the "misfortune" of owning their own business. Other rumors grew louder in and around Franklin County.

"I hope you're right with the Lord . . ."

The White Knights of the Mississippi Ku Klux Klan was a family affair for the Seales.[100] Descended from a line of local farmers and sawyers, sixty-four-year-old Clyde Wayne Seale was the exalted cyclops of the newly constituted Franklin County Klavern. His sons, Myron "Jack" and James, were also active members. So, too, was Charles Marcus Edwards, a thirty-one-year-old Korean War veteran. Edwards and his wife lived very close to Henry Hezekiah Dee, a nineteen-year-old Black teenager who worked at a local lumberyard. Known by his friends as "Pimp" for his conked hair, sharp dressing, and easy demeanor, Dee drew attention from local Klansmen for two other things: he traveled back and forth to Chicago to visit family, and he would often wear a black bandana to protect his pressed locks. In the fevered imagination of Edwards and other members of the Bunkley Klavern, Dee's trips north and his black do-rag could only signify one thing: he was running guns into Franklin County for the Black Muslims. Edwards mentioned Dee's suspicious activities at a Klan meeting in late April. As they'd done to other local Blacks who'd aroused their anger, enmity, and paranoia, the klavern would target Dee for a brutal beating, just to see what he might know.

Dee's friend Charles Eddie Moore, also nineteen and serving a temporary suspension from Alcorn A&M, had attended a Friday-night May Day dance at the local high school in Bude. The college freshman spent the night with his cousin Erbie Bell Shaw, who saw him off the following morning; he was wearing a Banlon sweater with blue jeans and sported a gold Bulova watch. His older brother, Thomas, a recent inductee into the US Army, had given him an "M" belt buckle as a birthday present. Later that morning, in Meadville, Moore met up with Dee, who'd spent part of his Saturday morning, May 2, stacking lumber at Wallace Jones's sawmill; the two agreed to hitch a ride back to Roxie. After cutting up with friend, Joey Rollins, in front of Dillon's gas station on Main Street, Moore and Dee waited for a ride.

Edwards initially spotted Dee in downtown Meadville at a local bank, and he quickly informed several Klansmen that Dee was on the move: now was their chance to take action against the feared gunrunning Black Muslim. James Ford Seale pulled up to the teenagers along Highway 84; upon spotting the white man in the white Volkswagen who seemed all too eager to offer them a ride, Moore and Dee withdrew their hands and politely declined Seale's offer. The twenty-nine-year-old truck-driving Klansman quickly grew irate and ordered the two into his car; he claimed to be an IRS "revenue agent" and wanted to talk to them about rumors of bootlegging. Moore and Dee's suspicions only increased when Seale communicated with a trailing pickup truck via two-way walkie-talkie. Their demands to be let out were ignored. Not far west of Meadville, Seale turned left and south to head deeper into the 189,000-acre Homochitto National Forest; the White Knights routinely used isolated hollows of the forest to beat Black men who'd attracted their suspicions.

Upon exiting the Volkswagen, and with other men spilling out of the pickup, Moore and Dee eyed an escape in the densely wooded forest, but

Seale and his sawed-off shotgun quickly dissuaded them. The teens were taken to a nearby tree, where their wrists were bound together with duct tape and their midsections tied to a nearby tree. The Klansmen found beanpoles—heavy but elastic wooden switches often used to stake green beans—and Edwards, Clyde Seale, and Curtis Dunn commenced the brutal whipping. They demanded to know where the Black Muslims were hiding guns in Franklin County, guns that would be used in that spring's resistance to Klan terrorism. Of course Moore and Dee had no idea what the men were talking about—and said as much. This only further enraged Seale, Edwards, and the other Klansmen. Bloodied and exhausted, Dee and Moore realized the truth wasn't going to get them out of the Homochitto Forest alive: the guns were being hidden at the Roxie Colored Baptist Church, pastored by the defiant Clyde Bennie Briggs, a World War II veteran, former schoolteacher, and local Black activist. And with that disclosure the brutal beating finally ended; Dee and Moore lapsed in and out of consciousness, soaked in blood and sweat from the fifteen minutes of Klan sadism.

Charles Edwards, Clyde Seale, and Archie Prather decided to head back to Meadville to track down the Franklin County sheriff in order to search the church. Before heading out of the forest, though, Edwards said to a barely conscious Henry Dee that he hoped Dee was "right with the Lord." Perhaps this not-so-veiled threat was Edwards's odd way of apologizing: the teenager whom he'd suspected of being a gunrunning radical Black Muslim was nothing of the sort; even a high school dropout like Edwards could divine that. Too, the faithful congregant at the Klan-infested Bunkley Baptist Church was also communicating to Dee that he knew he'd told the truth—at least for fourteen minutes. Why? Because if out-of-state guns were in fact found at the Roxie church, Moore and Dee could be tried for conspiracy; furthermore, any courtroom testimony by Moore or Dee against the Klansmen would fall on deaf ears in Franklin County. In brief, if the Klansmen found guns, Moore and Dee might be allowed to live; if no guns were discovered, a living Moore and Dee could pose all kinds of potential problems, including bringing COFO and its beatnik communist mixers into Franklin County. That a Klansman intent on murdering two innocent young Black men, and whose far-fetched conspiracy set the events of May 2 into motion, could invoke being "right with the Lord" is not without irony.

The Klansmen tracked down county sheriff Wayne Hutto and patrol-man Bernice Beasley (both rumored Klansmen) at the courthouse back in

Meadville. The officers quickly headed to Roxie, but the church was locked. They managed to locate Rev. Briggs at a friend's home in the tiny community of Crosby, nearly twenty miles south and west of Meadville. Once back at the Roxie Baptist Church, Hutto lied to Briggs that they were looking for a bomb, the church having purportedly been threatened. Despite ripping up floorboards and ransacking the church, no bombs (or guns) were found. Rev. Briggs later noted the curious search of the church in a journal he kept. As morning turned to afternoon, Clyde Seale and Prather dropped Edwards off at his home; Seale told him to keep his mouth shut and that everything would be taken care of. Edwards likely wondered if this false alarm, which would certainly lead to the murders of two innocent Black teenagers, and which he'd largely instigated, would be his own undoing with the Bunkley Klavern.

Moore and Dee clung to life, first in the back of James Ford Seale's white Volkswagen, and then in the trunk of Ernest Parker's red Ford. Seale, his brother Jack, and Dunn had driven the men from the Homochitto Forest, first to Clyde Seale's farm and later to an unknown location near Natchez, where Parker, a wealthy white landowner and fellow Klansman, agreed to drown the bodies in the Old River near his family's boat landing on Davis Island; nobody would think to even look for Moore and Dee in this remote place along the Mississippi-Louisiana line, more than eighty miles from Franklin County. And who would bother to look, anyway?

After crossing the Mississippi River at Natchez and heading north on Louisiana State Route 65, the lynching party arrived at the landing, still in Saturday's broad daylight. The Seale brothers and Parker moved quickly. Moore's and Dee's hands and feet were bound with hay wire, their mouths covered with duct tape. James Ford Seale argued that instead of shooting Moore and Dee before sinking them in the river, they'd simply drown the men using heavy engine and railroad parts near the landing; a bloody boat would leave too many clues. And so with no small effort, Parker and the Seale brothers chained heavy metals, including a Jeep engine block, to the torsos of the terrified young men. Charles Moore was forced to watch as his friend was dragged first into the low-drafting johnboat, navigated into the middle of the narrow river, and pushed overboard; the boat was simply too small to contain both men and the heavy anchors chained to their bodies. And so Charles Moore watched. He had to know as the day grew long that he was here in this lonely outpost only because he happened to make the mistake of hitching a ride with a friend; the Klan had absolutely nothing on him. Whether he thought of the possibility as his own horrifying death loomed, whether he could think at all, his jean pockets teemed with the quotidian items of his earthly existence. But in this terribly lonely stretch of wilderness, where bound and enslaved Africans once toiled under the broiling, humid sun on the Davis Plantation, would anyone ever find him? Them? . . .

Mazie Moore had seen her youngest son hitchhiking with Henry Dee that morning on her way to a doctor's appointment. But when Charles didn't return home she grew suspicious; she called Thelma Collins, Dee's sister, to inquire if she knew where the boys were. The call was Collins's first inkling that her brother might be in trouble. Three days later Mrs. Moore had grown worried enough to contact Franklin County sheriff Wayne Hutto. While the sheriff knew that Moore and Dee were both dead and at the bottom of the Old River, he told a distraught Mazie Moore that he'd heard the teenagers had traveled to relatives in Louisiana to find work for the summer. She and Thelma Collins headed to the relatives' home. Charles and Henry had not been there.

While Dave Webb continued to run ads soliciting membership for the Americans for the Preservation of the White Race in his weekly newspaper ahead of the Summer Project, the disappearance of two local teenagers did not rate so much as a mention in the *Franklin Advocate*. Nor did it rate as a missing persons case to be investigated by law enforcement, despite Mazie Moore and Thelma Collins's protestations. Whether or not Sheriff Hutto had directed Webb, a likely Klansman himself, not to report on the missing teens, suffice it to say that local news of Charles Moore and Henry Dee's whereabouts would only surface with the discovery of the partial remains of their bodies. For now official word had it that they were likely somewhere in Louisiana—which contained a horrifying measure of truth.

"... some sort of protection"

The governor's office in Jackson was "increasingly concerned" about the rise of the White Knights as well as the APWR in the southwestern part of the state. In office only four months, Governor Paul Johnson Jr. received a rather urgent "special report" from Erle Johnston, sovereignty commission director, on May 1, just the day before the kidnapping, beating, and murder of Moore and Dee. Johnston's contacts informed him that both groups were threatening "to take the laws into their own hands" and to smuggle in weapons from out of state. Further, Johnston had reliable sources inform him that both the Klan and the APWR were successfully recruiting state law enforcement into both organizations ahead of the coming "invasion."[101] In brief, the problem wasn't just a vigilante and violent Klan/APWR, but a coming confrontation in which vigilante white violence *was* the law.

As May began, bringing with it the realization that the Summer Project was really going to happen, Bob Moses began the most important letter-writing campaign of his career. During the campaign he enlisted anyone who might hold some sway with President Lyndon Johnson and his administration. On May 25, for example, he coauthored a letter with Aaron Henry and Dave Dennis, warning Johnson that the "violence and brutal resistance" visited upon Mississippians and civil rights workers "during the past three years" would likely intensify in four short weeks. Henry-Moses-Dennis had the temerity to request a face-to-face meeting with Johnson, going so far as suggesting dates.[102] Their offer was met with silence. But presidential silence didn't mean the administration wasn't listening—and making plans.

Later that same month, Claude Sitton's articles on the coming Summer Project for the *New York Times* were communicated with a bit more urgency: many were moved from the back pages to the front of the nation's newspaper of record. And, not surprisingly, violence was the principal subject. Specifically, in a May 30 page 1 story for the *Times*, Sitton noted that whites and Blacks in Mississippi shared the fear that "a summer-long drive involving hundreds of student volunteers from outside the state may lead to serious violence." Of course the violence wouldn't come from the students, nor even from white mobs protesting direct-action events such as the Freedom Day in Hattiesburg; rather, Sitton noted that the Ku Klux Klan had "experienced a resurgence" and that the main threat to volunteers would come "from isolated acts of terrorism, intimidation and harassment."[103] Just days later, and whether the cause was the reporting in national newspapers or the extensive lobbying by COFO and its affiliates, Lyndon Johnson was paying close attention to the threats of violence; so was his staff, including Robert Kennedy, attorney general, Nicholas Katzenbach, deputy attorney general, and Burke Marshall, assistant attorney general for civil rights. On

June 5, also on the front page of the *Times*, Hedrick Smith's lede noted that Johnson was "concerned about the possibility of violence this summer as civil rights protests spread throughout the country." The president and his staff had gone so far as to brainstorm privately the possibility of federal troops, as well as "methods of quiet persuasion."[104] Exacerbating the possibilities for white violence was the administration's looming, massive Civil Rights Act, which Johnson expected to sign as soon as late June or early July. A key provision of that bill would mandate the desegregation of all public accommodations, thus expanding the *Brown* school desegregation decision into the world of public commerce. In a word, the death rattles of state-sanctioned Jim Crow could be heard across the South as summer approached and as the Senate filibuster dragged on.

But publicly, the Johnson administration's cold shoulder to COFO worried its leadership, so much so that on June 8, Mississippi came to the nation's capital. Since the United States Commission on Civil Rights refused to hold open hearings in Mississippi, twenty-five Mississippians, including Fannie Lou Hamer and the widow of Louis Allen, Elizabeth Allen, testified at the National Theatre before a panel of writers, journalists, and academics about the horrors of Black life in Mississippi. The aim was to dramatize to the Johnson administration that federal protection was needed, as the Summer Project was less than two weeks away. Moses opened the hearing thus: "The purpose of this meeting is to try to open to the country and the world some of the facts which we who work in Mississippi only know too well," facts that haven't been "publicly aired and [are] very difficult to get across to the country."[105] Despite the harrowing testimony, despite an esteemed panel, and despite a transcript promptly entered into the *Congressional Record* by New York representative William Fitts Ryan, the all-day event seemed to fall on deaf ears: "Unfortunately, the effort proved unsuccessful. The Johnson administration paid no official public attention to the pleas, and the press gave little, if any, coverage of the event."[106] Not a word of the event was published in the *Times*, despite its extensive coverage of COFO's plans for the Summer Project.

Three days later, Dr. Harold Taylor, former president of Sarah Lawrence College and the chairman of the ad hoc citizens' committee that had listened to the testimony on June 8 in Washington, DC, wrote a two-page letter to the president. It began, "We, a group of citizens concerned with the increasing threat of violence and bloodshed in Mississippi, appeal to you to use now, and to the full, the administrative and executive powers which lie in your hands, to prevent the deaths and brutality which are sure to come to Mississippi this summer unless steps are taken to prevent them." Perhaps the most pressing power that Johnson could invoke was the power of presidential speech; specifically, the federal government needed to state its intentions to guarantee the personal safety of those in Mississippi, "Negro or white, residents or non-residents."[107] The logic was thoroughly rhetorical: a Johnson declaration would preempt violence directed at the summer volunteers. Of course the cagey Johnson was nobody's rhetorical fool; he well understood the complex dynamics of the situation. To make such a public declaration would concomitantly force his administration to commit to the volunteers' material protection—and this he wasn't willing to do. Not yet, anyway.

On the same day that Dr. Taylor's missive was mailed to the White House, Bob Moses decided to reemphasize to the summer volunteers just how urgent the situation was. Only three days before the start of training sessions at the Western College for Women in Oxford, Ohio,[108] Moses didn't mince words: all of their lives were imperiled—and the federal government needed to acknowledge this. The students ought to do the same. "It has occurred to us that we have perhaps not been forceful enough in impressing upon project workers the importance of alerting the federal government and local officials across the country of our plans for the next few months in Mississippi." Moses's finely calibrated conscience was clearly working overtime; doubt, and fear, (re)entered. While the federal government was aware that hundreds of volunteers would be in the state, "awareness is not enough. We must move our government to action." That action, Moses wrote, spoke to their collective safety: "We must insist that some sort of protection be provided for those hundreds of Americans who travel to Mississippi to work here within the grounds of their constitutional rights." He urged each volunteer "to appeal in every way possible" to senators, representatives, and local officials for federal protection. And once the volunteers were in Mississippi, their relatives, friends, and any "interested parties" should continue the lobbying campaign.[109]

Violence and the aims of the Summer Project were very much on SNCC's mind as training for the undertaking loomed. At a three-day SNCC staff meeting held in Atlanta on June 9–11, the gravity of what was at hand was first expressed by Mike Sayer, who asked: "How are we reacting to the possibilities of violence this summer?" Though he couched his message in a metaphor, Sayer understood that a new era was about to commence, and he wanted everyone assembled in Atlanta to recognize it: "This isn't just a large summer project, it's a war and for the first time we really have privates." While those white nonviolent privates might offer some level of protection, Moses quickly chimed in that the volunteers who would assemble shortly in Oxford must be made to understand the gravity of what they faced, that the "symbolic violence" of the past several years was also very real. Yet he also held out hope that violence might be somehow mitigated: "It's hard to say whether arbitrary acts of violence can be cut down. It's possible that recent violence . . . is just a last ditch attempt to scare off the summer project." Moses's optimism, however hedged, was immediately countered by Prathia Hall, who'd organized in Albany, Georgia. "No one can be rational about death. For the first time we are facing that this *may* be the last time. . . . When I discovered I was dead already I decided that I'd die to gain life." But possible death in Mississippi held profoundly rhetorical consequences for Hall: "We must bring the reality of our situation to the nation. Bring our blood on to the [W]hite [H]ouse door. If we die here it's the whole society which has pulled the trigger by its silence." Sayer jumped back into the conversation: "The way the situation exists now whites know that violence is the most sensible way of getting us." The following day, the final staff meeting before Oxford and then Mississippi, the specter of violence returned. Lawrence Guyot echoed and extended Moses from the previous day: Volunteers must know that "our only protection now is militancy. . . . If you are worried about protecting yourself you must leave." Charles McLaurin had the final word at the meeting about violence and the purpose of the project. Just three days prior, on his way to Atlanta, McLaurin and several Black SNCC colleagues had been badly beaten by police officers in Lowndes County, Mississippi. The still-recovering McLaurin's question was eerily prescient: "What are we trying do, develop Freedom Schools and work on voter registration or get the federal government involved and open the eyes of the nation? If the latter is our goal perhaps we should send whites into new communities where violence will occur."[110]

"... a media summer"

The summer volunteers began arriving in Oxford, Ohio, on the weekend of June 13. After all the debate, the endless planning, the frenetic recruitment efforts, and the late cancellation by Berea College for hosting the orientation sessions, the young white men and women came. So, too, did the press, lots of them. SNCC staffers in particular could spot the volunteers from across the bucolic campus: clad in chinos, collared shirts, and print dresses, America's finest looked like they were headed to brunch at the local country club rather than the dusty back roads and swamps of Mississippi. The SNCC staff wore their work shirts, overalls, and boots; no sense stepping out of uniform now. Their pride was also unmistakable. To many of the summer volunteers, COFO staffers were decidedly not warm and inviting; in fact, many seemed downright hostile. Sitton observed that "the professionals also indicate their resentment, in guarded terms, at the necessity of turning to amateurs for assistance in the Mississippi project."[111] That hostility and resentment boiled over into open anger quickly. At a screening of the CBS documentary *Mississippi and the 15th Amendment*, the college kids laughed at the opening visage of Forrest County registrar Theron Lynd. Shot in mocking profile, the massively corpulent and crew-cut Lynd looked exactly like the Southern caricature: fat, white, and flat-topped. The staff saw a completely different visage: This was the evil in Hattiesburg that they'd contended with back in January at the Freedom Day event, and who continued to flaunt a federal court's injunction to register local Black voters. What could possibly be funny? Several staff fled the hall in disgust. Bob Moses tried to explain.[112]

He also tried to explain it to Lyndon Johnson just one more time. The Harvard-trained philosopher with a penchant for the French existentialists had to be both thrilled and deeply worried. Thrilled because the dream—uniquely his dream—of Freedom Summer was finally upon him and his staff. If Mississippi could be cracked open and finally brought into the Union, this interracial and nonviolent army would do what he and his meager staff couldn't do. Worried because this wasn't the Freedom Vote, and the White Knights had loudly announced their presence—not just in Franklin County and the southwest, but all over the state. And in the fevered imagination of the Mississippi racist, stoked by months of dire warnings of invasion, beatnik interracial orgies, and communism, a "n-----lover" was way worse than a "n-----." Any day. The president had refused to issue a public warning to Mississippians, had refused to make a public speech, hold a press conference; he had refused to meet with civil rights leaders—had refused even to acknowledge publicly the existence of the Summer Project. And so Moses cut to the chase: "We are requesting that the Negroes of Mississippi and the summer volunteers receive Federal protection. This may require the stationing of members of the Department of Justice in Mississippi for the summer, sending special teams of F.B.I. members into the state, stationing Federal Marshalls [sic], or even, in the event of a complete breakdown of law, sending in Federal troops." Moses had to wonder why the president was being so obtuse; after all, these were the nation's white elite. Didn't the federal government have an almost statutory obligation to protect them? "Whatever the case, we are asking you to give protection for the Negroes of Mississippi and the civil rights workers in the state."[113] And with that, Bob Moses's pre-project letter-writing campaign to the president of the United States ended. He had tried everything he knew to defuse the impending violence. Blood—white or Black blood—would not be just on his hands this time.

Stokely Carmichael could hardly believe all the press that had descended on the small southwestern Ohio community. Then again, his incredulities waned just as soon as he watched them in action: the press was interested in one and only one story—and it had nothing to do with Black COFO staff. "They ran through the campus looking for photogenic 'all-American' types for interviews. Some networks even selected subjects to follow up during the summer. I can't recall that a single staff or local leader was so selected. Nor even a Northern Black volunteer."[114] While Carmichael found it "odd" that the press would favor a pimply nineteen-year-old white sophomore over Fannie Lou Hamer, he also knew that the white press, its white subjects, and its white readers were doing precisely what many in COFO wanted and predicted: namely, generating national publicity and (hopefully) the protection such publicity would engender. Len Edwards, a white nineteen-year-old sophomore at the University of California, later noted, "The Mississippi summer was a media summer. . . . I was a media person. . . . just being there brought our families with us."[115] Said another white volunteer: "We're not dupes. . . . I am being used, but I know why and how, and will that Bob Moses so use me."[116] Of course it didn't hurt that

Edwards's father was a prominent California congressman, Don Edwards; the elder Edwards would cause a media stir when he visited the project in July. And yet, that racial calculus, which valued white life in ways that Blacks could only resent, did nothing for the interracial solidarity at Oxford.

". . . completely fed up with these do-gooders"

By Wednesday morning, June 17, word had gotten back to Mickey Schwerner and James Chaney, both in Oxford, that several members of the Mt. Zion Methodist Church had been brutally assaulted by hooded Klansmen the night before; they'd hoped to find "Goatee," their code name for the whiskered Schwerner, at Mt. Zion. The church was burned to the ground just hours later; there would be no Freedom School at this site in Neshoba County. He and JE agreed to leave Oxford a bit early in order to visit Mt. Zion on Sunday, June 21, and try to reassure its parishioners. Rita Schwerner would head back later, as she would be helping train volunteers during the second week. Schwerner and Chaney decided to bring back with them to Meridian a twenty-year-old junior-to-be at Queens College, Andy Goodman. Originally slated to organize in the relatively peaceful city of Vicksburg, Goodman had agreeably signed on with Schwerner (a fellow New Yorker) and Chaney.

The three pulled out of Oxford at 3:00 a.m. on Saturday. The same day, a somewhat familiar white face appeared on campus: John Doar, from the Johnson Justice Department, where he worked as deputy chief in the department's Civil Rights Division. Doar had served with no small bravery in several tense scenes, most recently at the near-riot in Jackson following the funeral for Medgar Evers. Whether or not Doar's appearance was Johnson's ostensible response to Bob Moses's constant lobbying, all of the Summer Project staff and volunteers were keen to hear what official Washington had to say. To the assembled 275 men and women, Doar confessed his admiration for the work the students had undertaken and were undertaking: "The real heroes in this country today," Sitton of the *Times* reported, "are the students," particularly those who'd taken on the "very bad and evil problems in the South." But during the question and answer session, responding to a very pointed question about whether the volunteers could expect federal protection, Doar didn't mince words: no federal police force would be there to protect them.[117] Period. "You could feel a sudden, palpable deflation in that room," recalled Stokely Carmichael.[118] And then, loud jeering and booing broke out in Peabody Hall. Bob Moses quickly intervened: "We don't do that," he implored. The Black COFO staff might have snickered at the official rebuke of white privilege and its incredulous reaction. Nobody apparently thought to ask the deputy chief the next logical question: Would the federal government intervene if one of them went missing, or was beaten, kidnapped, or murdered? And just what would it take to get the Johnson administration actively involved in Mississippi? Sitton closed his article by noting the formation of the rather unwieldily named Parents Emergency Committee for Federal Protection of Students in the Mississippi Summer Project." Its founder, Kaye Raphael, hoped to "force intervention before an incident occurs."

The assembled press pounced on the Doar remark: "Of all the speeches the press heard that day," noted Carmichael, "that statement of Doar's became *the* story across the country." Far more problematic to Carmichael and COFO was how Doar's statement played in Mississippi: "The federal government was now signaling its intention to stand aside, freeing the good people of Mississippi to defend their 'way of life' by whatever means necessary." Carmichael went further: Regardless of intent, Doar's statement "seemed to imply federal license to murder. For some socially marginal good ol' boy, subject to months of demagogic incitement, that would have seemed a patriotic duty. And a clear signal."[119] Carmichael's sagacious bit of rhetorical criticism was also echoed by a back-page and un-bylined piece in the *Times* published on June 21. Carmichael's "good ol' boy" was the more measured *Times's* "average citizen." But both had been primed by a relentless onslaught in the white Mississippi press and by the state's politicians. He "has been lead to believe that this will be an 'invasion' to make Mississippi the battleground for federal intervention in behalf of Negro rights." Further, the *Times* claimed that he "knows only what staunchly segregationist newspapers and politicians have said about the registration project." The closed society of Mississippi, recently limned by Ole Miss professor James Silver in a book by the same name, ominously awaited: "He believes it spells violence and bloodshed, and he may be right."[120]

If the *New York Times* was reading a broad swath of the white Mississippi press as the volunteers came south, the registers seemed to be three: total indifference, righteous anger, and calculated restraint. Many small-town weeklies simply ignored the coming invaders and the accompanying press; they dutifully reported far more important news items such as agricultural outlooks, obituaries, social news, and—always—the latest beauty pageant results. Other papers, often smaller-circulation weeklies, showed little if any restraint. "Outsiders who come in here," opined the *Neshoba Democrat*, "and try to stir up trouble should be dealt with in a manner they won't forget."[121] The editor of the *Woodville Republican* was fed up before the project even commenced, "We're completely fed up with these do-gooders from hither and yon and the efforts to bring the blessings of their kind of society to us poor benighted Mississippians."[122] The *Jackson Advocate*, owned and operated by Percy Greene, a Black man and paid informant for the white-supremacist Sovereignty Commission, adopted a common Mississippi response: "Without condoning racist attitudes, we think it understandable if people in Mississippi should resent such an invasion. The outsiders are said to regard themselves as some sort of heroic freedom fighters, but in truth they are asking for trouble."[123] Much like the "provocatively dressed" rape victim, summer volunteers were asking for a violent confrontation by dint of their pro–civil rights mission. But the sartorial and the particulars of that mission were rarely far apart among the fevered: many were "ill kempt," "bearded and barefoot," with a penchant for folk singing; "one of the girls (white) was described as having heels so rusty they looked like rooster spurs."[124] And Dave Webb published in his weekly *Franklin Advocate* a "sound" piece by the Leake County *Carthaginian*'s publisher, George Keith, who wanted "to vomit. . . . It is absolutely sickening to see these freakish people as they mingle among the Negroes."[125] White Mississippians likely took note of the not-so-subtle dog whistle: "Mingling" was code for interracial sex, and for many editors, the whole Summer Project was a very thinly veiled communist-inspired interracial orgy. At the Holly Springs *South Reporter* those links were made explicit: "Most Civil Rights organizations stress the point that they do not wish to see intermarriage between the races but the social behavior of the workers here obviously reflects their approval of it. Or else it's something done just for 'kicks' while they are down here. Their dress alone is enough to convince all right-thinking people, white or colored, that they will be unable to teach anyone higher ideals or morals."[126]

Many editors took a slightly different rhetorical approach with their readers; instead of encouraging violence, they counseled caution. If white

Mississippians would simply ignore the "invaders," all would return to normal in a mere two months. In brief, many attempted to communicate the rhetorical calculus: violence perpetrated on the volunteers would bring a federal response, and it would only feed an already frenzied national press, thus heaping further calumny on the state. That so many in the Mississippi press felt compelled to make such an urgent demand is also a revealing barometer of how armed and angry so many white Mississippians were. Some publishers and editors might have concluded that their appeals would be too little too late: The press and the politicians had simply stoked the collective anger and outrage for too long; an editorial, however rational and well argued, was not going to cool a white-hot rage brought to a rolling boil over nearly eight long months. But many tried.

The *Neshoba Democrat* attempted to walk back its earlier sentiments: "It is important that we restrain ourselves and give them no reason for creating situations that we will all be sorry of in the future. . . . This will probably be the longest and the hardest summer any of us has ever spent, and there's no use to make it any worse by popping off when restraint will get the job done better." Residents could rest easy knowing that "we think we have duly elected officials capable of handling the situation."[127] The equivocation—"we think"—is most suggestive; one such official was county sheriff Lawrence Rainey, who'd already killed two Black men during his duties as a police officer in Neshoba. On its front page, the *Greenwood Commonwealth* urged the citizens of Leflore County, "If every citizen, white and Black, does his part to see that law prevails during the next two months, September will find Mississippi the same 2,000,000 people it has always been."[128] Greenwood in particular would be in the media glare, as SNCC had temporarily moved its national headquarters from Atlanta to the Delta and the Long Staple Cotton Capital of the World. The *Commonwealth* also reprinted, on the same day and in the same edition, an editorial from the *Clarksdale Press Register*. While there was much to resent in "this summer-long program, there is nothing to justify intemperate action or reaction on the part of any citizen of Clarksdale, the Delta or Mississippi." The *Press Register* also noted the potential economic consequences of violence, quoting the president of the Mississippi Economic Council, Balmer Hill: "It is imperative that we conduct ourselves with dignity, poise, forbearance, and, if possible, even good humor. We should not gather into curious crowds or allow ourselves to be provoked into impulsive acts that would reflect discredit to our state."[129] Two days later, in an editorial titled "The People and the Intruders," the *Press Register* again counseled restraint: "We can use our heads, or we can lose our heads—and the only possible success that can come to our tormentors would be for us to lose our heads and indulge in words or actions which would focus unwarranted attention in our direction." Surely, the editor implored, we "can manage to accommodate and ignore for two months this pitiful influx of 300 to 500 beatnik sophomores and motley missionaries."[130] And in his page 1 "City Meddler" column, the editor at the *Indianola Enterprise-Tocsin* also urged caution: "It is true that they would like nothing better than to cause some sort of disturbance to bring down the Feds on us and all of us be put under Marshall [*sic*] Law. This could happen if we fail to keep our heads."[131]

Among the blizzard of newspaper voices in Mississippi, one stood out for its willingness to confront the state's extremists. Many Mississippians could not have been surprised: Hodding Carter Jr., since taking ownership of the *Delta Democrat-Times*, hard by the levees of the western Delta community of Greenville, had consistently pitched a relatively progressive racial message. Winner of the 1946 Pulitzer Prize for his editorializing on race, Carter—the "braying jackass," as one state legislator called him—was often in the crosshairs of the state's white supremacists. The Bowdoin-educated World War II veteran and son of the South would not be cowed by popular white public opinion as Freedom Summer commenced. He editorialized that the Black Chicago comedian and civil rights activist Dick Gregory predicted that up to seventy-five Summer Project volunteers might die; only then might the "American conscience" be prodded to protect them. Carter counseled that the summer was "a time for thinking. It is a time to wait, to hope, and to pray."[132] Two days later and Carter's tune seemed to change: "There is at last a chance for equal combat against our homegrown totalitarians—tragically late, but present nonetheless. Let us not miss the opportunity because of inertia, apathy or cowardice. The shackles of fear which have for so long bound white as well as Negro can be removed once and for all, if the good people will at last join those who have now taken the lead in the attempt."[133]

The homegrown totalitarians might have also gotten the attention of the powerful Mississippi senator John Stennis. While his outspoken and openly racist fellow senator James O. Eastland seemed to attract most of the headlines, Stennis tried for something of a Hail Mary as the Civil Rights

Act of 1964 careened toward Lyndon Johnson's desk.[134] On June 12, the junior senator offered a friendly amendment to the bill, what some called the "anti–Freedom Rider amendment," which sought to make it a federal offense to cross state lines or send someone across state lines in order to violate a state law. If passed, perhaps the amendment would force COFO's hand, since the state of Mississippi had passed a flurry of anti–civil rights bills in the spring. Whether Stennis's motive was to scuttle the Summer Project for fear of imminent violence or something less altruistic, his fellow senators quickly voted down the amendment, seventy-two to twenty-one. A week later the sweeping Civil Rights Act, more than a year in the making, passed the Senate, seventy-three to twenty-seven. Desegregation and new voting provisions were coming to Mississippi just as soon as Johnson signed the bill into law.

Imminent and lethal violence is what Sam Bowers preached from deep in the woods just two weeks before the Summer Project officially launched. From the pulpit at Boykin Methodist Church, near the small central Mississippi community of Raleigh, the thirty-nine-year-old Bowers outlined the White Knights' "Christian" battle plan. Bowers opened his speech, "Fellow Klansmen, you know why we are here. We are here to discuss what we are going to do about COFO's n----- communist invasion of Mississippi which will begin in a few days." Bowers held aloft a lengthy "Imperial Executive Order," which he proceeded to read to the two hundred Klansmen assembled from around the state: "The military and political situation as regards the enemy has now reached the crisis stage. Our best students of enemy strategy and technique"—most likely the exceedingly self-righteous Bowers—"are in almost complete agreement that the events which will occur in Mississippi this summer may well determine the fate of Christian civilization for centuries to come." How a few hundred white kids on college break working on a voter registration drive, providing summer tutoring, and playing interracial ping-pong at a local community center could engender The Apocalypse beggars the imagination. But, the White Knights' deeply paranoid worldview could quickly translate interracial contact as sex that always teetered on the knife-edge of rape; cross-racial voting as governmental overthrow; and the National Council of Churches as a communist and atheist front. Bowers stressed that the White Knights must never enter into "daylight conflict" with the enemy or appear as an unruly "mob"; rather, under the cover of darkness, they must work with local law enforcement to secure both legitimacy and cover: "Our first contact with the troops of the enemy in the streets should be as legally deputized law enforcement officers." Bowers further specified that these law enforcement officials should come "from our own ranks." With the "when" taken care of, Bowers detailed exactly who should be attacked, and how: "Any personal attacks on the enemy should be carefully planned to include only the leaders and prime white collaborators of the enemy forces." Did that include death? "These attacks against these selected individual targets should, of course, be as severe as circumstances and conditions will permit."[135] William Bradford Huie, one of the first reporters on the ground following the June 21 disappearance, claims that a "number 4"—an extermination order—for Mickey Schwerner was in place by mid-May. Further, the Lauderdale Klavern was not authorized to make the hit; it didn't have "strong enough" ties to local law enforcement. The Neshoba Klavern, though, did: both Sheriff Lawrence Rainey and his deputy, Cecil Price, were active members.[136]

Sam Bowers had issued from the pulpit of Boykin Methodist nothing short of "a declaration of war against COFO."[137] The White House, the Justice Department, FBI headquarters, and Mississippi law enforcement each had a copy of the Imperial Executive Order within hours; the White Knights of Mississippi had, it seemed, at least one Judas in its midst.

"Sir, I know just how you feel . . ."

The events of June 21, 1964, are, in the words of the dean of Mississippi civil rights historians, John Dittmer, "the most depressingly familiar story of the Mississippi movement."[138] I'll return to that characterization in a later section. But many Americans know the events of that day—the victims, the suspects, the places, even the chronology—because Bob Moses and COFO had been dead-on in their initial assessment: the country would only care about Mississippi if COFO brought it there; more specifically, white America would only care about Black Mississippians when its white sons and daughters turned up missing and presumed dead. "Plenty of Negroes had suffered violence," observed the American writer Robert Penn Warren, "So you do not get intervention by violence as such. You get it by violence to white skin."[139] Visser-Maessen notes that already in its first week, "COFO had already largely accomplished what it sought to achieve. . . . it invited white retaliation, but [the murders'] effect on a national audience paradoxically inhibited new violence."[140]

The three young men had, in fact, taken the Neshoba Klavern's bait: Goodman, Schwerner, and Chaney drove the thirty-five miles north to the Longdale community on the morning of June 21 to investigate the immolation of Mt. Zion Methodist Church.[141] Before departing the Meridian Community Center, Schwerner informed Sue Brown, then in charge of the office, that they would be back by 4:00 p.m. If for some reason they weren't, she was instructed to start making calls at 4:30. After getting the blue 1963 Ford Fairlane station wagon serviced by a Black-owned shop in Meridian, and getting haircuts, the men were off; James Chaney drove. They were all still tired, having driven close to seventeen hours the previous day. On the sunny, warm day, the longest of the year, the men first stopped at the home of Earnest Kirkland, perhaps the most important contact Mickey and JE had developed in the Longdale community. They then stopped at the burned-out remains of Mt. Zion, visited next with Cornelius Steele and his wife Mavis, who'd been accosted by the Klan on June 16, then headed over to interview Junior Roosevelt "Bud" Cole and his wife, Beatrice. The fifty-eight-year-old deacon still bore the scars of the vicious beating he'd taken on Tuesday night; his wife's timely prayer likely saved his life. The three men next stopped at Georgia Rush's place, but she wasn't home. At Kirkland's invitation, the final stop in Longdale they made was at his parents' home; it was getting on toward 3:00.

There are, of course, countless what-ifs in the Philadelphia story, but one of the most beguiling is the route the men decided to take home. Headed south on Longdale Drive toward the major east/west intersection of Highway 16, JE made a right and headed toward Philadelphia, where they would pick up Highway 19 and travel south back to Meridian. A left on Highway 16 would have taken the men to County Road 492, which bypassed Philadelphia altogether. The men's fate was inexorably sealed with that right turn; lurking in town was Deputy Sheriff Cecil Price, who had been on the lookout for the blue Fairlane with the license plate H 25 503. The Sovereignty Commission had provided local law enforcement with the tag number. Nearly into town, in front of First United Methodist Church, the Fairlane's back right tire was found to be flat.[142] As the men got out to change it, Price's two-toned Chevy police car pulled up behind them with its flashing lights on. Chaney was under arrest for doing 65 in a

35 mph zone; Goodman and Schwerner were under arrest for suspicions of conspiracy in the burning of Mt. Zion. Highway patrolmen Earle Poe and W. J. Wiggins had been radioed to assist with the arrest.

Unbeknown to the three civil rights workers, from the moment, nearing 4:00, that they were booked into the Neshoba County Jail by Minnie Lee Herring, things began moving very quickly among Price's fellow Klansmen. The architect of the plan was Edgar Ray Killen, who lived south of Philadelphia in Union. Calls went out to fellow Klansmen and the plan was put into motion: Price would deliver the three men under the cover of darkness after they were released from the county jail, somewhere along Highway 19; the bodies would be taken to the Old Jolly Farm that Olen Burrage owned, and on which he was constructing a large dam to hold a cow pond with two Cat D4 bulldozers. Burrage was said to have boasted that the large dam "could hold a hundred of 'em." Under twenty feet of Neshoba's red clay soil on rural private property, the bodies would never be unearthed.

Minnie Lee's husband, Virgil Herring, offered to make a call on Schwerner's behalf to his wife, Rita. For several possible reasons, Schwerner politely declined the offer; the Herrings didn't appear to be in on the White Knights' conspiracy.[143] Regardless, Schwerner was confident that Sue Brown and her colleagues back in Meridian were just then frantically calling local law enforcement trying to locate the tardy men, per carefully rehearsed protocol. As the clock neared 10:00 and the sun finally set on this longest day, surely the FBI would have already been alerted; perhaps even a nearby attorney would inquire about them. Would John Doar still be in Oxford?

Near 10:30, Cecil Price reappeared; he claimed to have finally found the justice of the peace to set the terms of their release. The men were free to go once Schwerner paid the twenty-dollar speeding fine; Mrs. Herring gave them a receipt. Price walked the men to their car, carefully steering them away from the lobby of the nearby Benwalt Hotel, where there was a pay phone: "Now, let's see how quickly y'all can get out of Neshoba County," Price glowered. To emphasize that he was not playing, Price's patrol car patiently followed the Ford Fairlane wagon as it zigged and zagged through Philadelphia on the way over to Highway 19—the only direct way back home to Meridian. And with Price finally out of sight, perhaps the three men shared an extended exhale; it had been a long and stressful day in the hundred-plus-degree temperatures, the isolation, and the uncertainty.

Did the men keep an eye out for a pay phone, even as the year's longest day went dark?

Near the tiny community of House, just a few miles south of town, James Chaney noticed in his rearview mirror a line of cars coming at them fast. A very skilled driver with a powerful car, he decided to make a run for the Lauderdale County line. As speeds reached over one hundred miles per hour, Chaney dove to his right onto County Road 492, a dirt road that intersected with Highway 15 just east of Union. Price was closely in pursuit and hit his flashing lights. For unknown reasons, Chaney stopped the car. Price ordered the men out of the Fairlane and back into his patrol car. Klansmen got into the COFO car and the caravan headed back out to Highway 19, then slowly north toward Philadelphia. Cecil Price never testified to what the three men said or did, but they likely knew their lives were in grave danger. Perhaps the men resorted to their training in Gandhian principles: try to establish some bond, however thin, to a shared humanity; even riotous Klansmen could be reached, as Rev. Ed King had relayed to Mickey in Ohio.[144] At Rock Cut Road, also known as County Road 515, Price turned left, followed closely by the caravan of vehicles, including the blue Fairlane. At the intersection of County Roads 515 and 284, and sheltered by the high red walls of a ravine, Price stopped and cut the engine; the other cars did the same. Klansman Alton Wayne Roberts, a hulking former football player, moved quickly to the police cruiser, pulled open the left rear door, and yanked out Mickey Schwerner, who made one last attempt: "Sir, I know just how you feel." With that Roberts squeezed off a round, point-blank, into Schwerner's heart. He crumpled into the ditch. Roberts next grabbed Goodman and executed him in near identical manner. James Jordan, who would later turn informant, wanted in on the action; he opened the right rear door and grabbed Chaney, who tried to ascend the steep bank. Jordan shot him in the abdomen, leaving him lying on the ground; Roberts put one bullet in Chaney's back and a final kill-shot to his brain.

Jimmy Arledge had lowered the tailgate on the Fairlane; the bleeding bodies were quickly piled in. Knowing that the five pistol shots not far from Highway 19 would attract attention, the posse quickly moved out: Price headed back to the night shift at the sheriff's office while Billy Posey drove the blue station wagon north and west to Indian Road, not far from Philadelphia and very close to its famous Neshoba Fairgrounds. There, as planned, they entered the isolated 253-acre Jolly Farm; waiting for them was the bulldozer operator, Herman Tucker. The powerful Cat D4 and its skillful operator made quick work of the burial: a narrow notch was cut near the middle of the dam and the bodies dragged in. Whereas Mississippi had long been infamous for its swamps, bayous, and rivers as final hiding places for Black lynching victims, the twenty-one coconspirators weren't going to take any chances on these three bodies being found. Whiteness was special, even more so in death.

Before the Summer Project had even really begun, Bob Moses's worst fears—the very fears he'd publicly articulated for months—had become a reality. The supposed on-off violence switch of the Freedom Vote must have lingered now like a bad hallucination. As he later confessed, he and the COFO staff knew by Monday that the men were dead. But what remained to be seen was how both the press and the federal government would respond to the disappearance, especially given the near-constant warnings they'd received for the past three months. Moses and COFO had clearly lost the early round in this perilous high-stakes rhetorical contest; the White Knights did exactly what they claimed they would do, and the feds had not budged. What now? As they headed to Mississippi and their projects, staffers such as George Greene, Hollis Watkins, Willie Peacock, even Bob Moses's wife, Dona, likely knew the rough outline of what would follow. Had Charles Moore and Henry Dee even been reported as missing yet? Even worse, COFO didn't even know to know that two Black Mississippians—seven weeks on—had also been abducted by the White Knights.

"... and she wouldn't play"

The responses by both the press and the federal government to the missing activists were swift, massive, and unprecedented. The first big break in the case came on Monday morning, June 22, when Minnie Lou Herring confirmed that the three men had been in her jail Sunday afternoon and evening, and that they'd been freed at 10:30 Sunday night. FBI agents were on the ground in Philadelphia by the afternoon, ordered by US attorney general Robert Kennedy to make a full inquiry. The use of military equipment was authorized and approved by President Johnson. The first story about the disappearance hit the *New York Times*'s front page on the 23rd; for the next forty-two days, thirty-eight stories about the three men would be published in the nation's newspaper of record, many of them on page 1. But the *Times* was far from the only interested media outlet; as Roberts and Klibanoff note, almost overnight, Philadelphia, Mississippi, "had become one of the most prominent datelines in the world."[145]

Sitton's first story on the disappearance is instructive on several levels. He describes the escalating violence in Mississippi ahead of Freedom Summer; he notes that the FBI was already on the ground in Neshoba County; and he quotes the two lawmen around whom suspicions would swirl for several months: Deputy Sheriff Cecil Price and Sheriff Lawrence Rainey. The latter, described by Sitton as a "burly, tobacco-chewing man," adopted the line that many white Mississippians, including the state's senior senator, would use for the next six weeks: "If they're missing, they just hid somewhere, trying to get a lot of publicity out of it, I figure."[146] Clearly Sheriff Rainey had been reading the Mississippi press and the long-running attribution of motive: the battle for public opinion had been officially joined.

In a revealing phone conversation with Lyndon Johnson on June 22, an incredulous Senator Eastland argued, "I don't believe there's three missing. I believe it's a publicity stunt. . . . I don't think there's a damn thing to it." The chair of the Judiciary Committee's profane disbelief stemmed from one basic "fact": there was no organized resistance in eastern Mississippi—no Klan and no Citizens' Councils. "Who could possibly harm them? There's nobody in that area to harm them." While Eastland confessed that in other parts of the state—clearly referring to the southwestern area—such harm could be real, his credulities did not extend to Neshoba and Lauderdale Counties. And while the senator and the president talked with jovial familiarity about the dry spell harming the cotton crop in Texas and Mississippi, the wily former senate majority leader coyly let Eastland know that an epic shitstorm was headed to his state: "Several weeks ago, I asked them [FBI] to anticipate the problems that would come from this [Summer Project]."[147] Reflecting Hedrick Smith's article in the *Times* from June 5, which had noted Johnson's concern about the possibility of violence, the Moses-led lobbying campaign was beginning to bear fruit. Later on the same day, Johnson and Eastland agreed that the president would send to Mississippi a federal proxy to seek information and publicly get Mississippi's commitment to enforce the law. That proxy would also carry to Governor Johnson and Attorney General Patterson the FBI's list of Mississippi lawmen who were members of the Ku Klux Klan.

Johnson had other pressing rhetorical matters to consider. The parents of the two missing white men were in Washington, DC, and seeking a meeting with him. Should Johnson meet with them and thus potentially bring every worried Freedom Summer parent into the Oval Office? He answered his own question: they could meet with a presidential proxy instead. Whether it was afternoon news from the Bogue Chitto Swamp or some other source of persuasion, Johnson quickly changed his mind and decided to meet with Nathan Schwerner and Carolyn and Robert Goodman himself. As she met with the president, Carolyn Goodman was surprised to learn that the 1963 Ford Fairlane had turned up near a Choctaw Indian reservation just off of Highway 21 north and east of Philadelphia. The burned-out husk, still smoldering, carried no bodies and few clues, J. Edgar Hoover reported. Johnson quickly dispatched more than one hundred sailors from the naval air station in Meridian to search the swamp for clues. Or bodies. Perhaps both.

Back in Franklin County, Mazie Moore and Thelma Collins couldn't get sheriff Wayne Hutto to even classify their son and brother as missing. The Black teenagers must still be somewhere in Louisiana looking for work.

Not surprisingly, it would take a white woman activist—perhaps a white widow—to draw the connection, however implicit, between the events in Franklin County and Neshoba County. The immediate national media and federal response did not surprise her; in fact, she clearly anticipated it. But instead of ignoring the issue, instead of playing the role of a weepy and diffident spouse pining for her husband, Rita Schwerner launched her own rhetorical campaign. SNCC organizer Dorothy Zellner recounted, "The press swarmed all over her, and I think they wanted her to cry, and they wanted her to be a new widow, that they would catch her at the moment of hew new widowhood, and she wouldn't play."[148] Within hours of learning of her husband's disappearance, she was in Philadelphia to confront Sheriff Rainey and demanded to see the burned-out Fairlane; she next went to Jackson and confronted a horrified Paul Johnson, who literally ran from her into the safety of the governor's mansion; she then headed to Washington, DC, and informed the taken-aback president that she wasn't in town to make a "social call," but to demand answers about the three men's disappearance. Rita's anger and lack of deference and decorum so alarmed and rankled Johnson that he could only understand her "ugly" theatrics as that of someone "worse than a communist." Before print journalists as well as television cameras, Rita Schwerner laid bare the nation's racial logic: "We all know that this search with hundreds of sailors is because Andrew Goodman and my husband are white. If only Chaney was involved, nothing would've been done."[149] Before a different set of cameras and journalists, she again impugned the assembled media: "I personally suspect that if Mr. Chaney, who is a native Mississippian Negro, had been alone at the time of the disappearance, that this case, like so many that have come before, would've gone completely unnoticed."[150] Rather than lamenting her personal loss, Rita Schwerner contextualized the massive media presence and the enormous and rapid federal response as premised on only one variable: skin color. And even as she made her pointed critique, Schwerner likely understood a telling irony: her remarks about white privilege and access were given credence by virtue of her own whiteness. As Bruce Watson notes, "Never had a disappearance in the Deep South sent such tremors through the nation. The alarm also paid unwelcome tribute to the planners of Freedom Summer. Their cynicism had been dead on. All the Blacks murdered in Mississippi since Emmett Till had scarcely raised concerns beyond state borders."[151]

On Thursday evening, June 25, CBS aired an hour-long prime-time program, *The Search in Mississippi*, anchored by Walter Cronkite. Two days later, NBC broadcast its own *Special Report: Chaney, Goodman and Schwerner*. Media continued to pour into Neshoba County as the search for the three men spread beyond the Bogue Chitto Swamp and into the Pearl River. President Johnson's proxy, former director of the Central Intelligence Agency Allen Dulles, met with Mississippi state officials and gathered evidence for the president. His conclusion? The federal government needed to send in more help. FBI director J. Edgar Hoover advocated for federal marshals. Johnson sagaciously pointed out that such "troops" would remind Mississippians of Oxford and the lethal integration of Ole Miss. No, he wanted to send more FBI—and he also wanted to send the director. He also told the director rather pointedly, whenever the Klan opened its mouth, he wanted to know what was said. Thus began a massive influx of FBI agents into Mississippi, capped by the director's press conference at the brand-new FBI headquarters in Jackson on July 10.[152]

COFO had its own human intelligence it was pursuing on the ground in and around Neshoba County. Even as they acknowledged that they were now looking for bodies, Stokely Carmichael, Charles Cobb, Cleveland

Sellers, and several others quietly snuck into town. Housed by landowning Black families, the men searched the lonely countryside under the cover of darkness: in abandoned wells, shallow swamps, and rumored Klan hideouts, the men searched in vain for their three colleagues. They eventually abandoned Neshoba County; they had to get to their projects and the hard work of the summer. A second wave of white college students was on its way south.[153]

Despite frequent exhortations, many white Mississippians had not gotten the message from local newspaper editors: calls for restraint, physical and otherwise, had gone unheeded. And because of that, the federal government and the national press had set up camp in their state; it was precisely the situation that so many had feared all along. The Goodman, Schwerner, and Chaney story would "brand us before the world, with the enthusiastic help of the liberal press, as a barbaric people," the *Vicksburg Evening-Post* lamented.[154] The *Woodville Republican* could not understand the "hullabaloo [that] has been raised throughout the nation over the disappearance of the three civil rights workers from the Philadelphia area last week." While the paper claimed it was likely a "huge hoax" designed to bring the press and the federal government into the state, the national attention made no sense: "What we cannot understand, no matter what the fate of the three men, is why the incident should prove to be banner headline news throughout the nation day after day." Their rage was barely contained, "We're completely fed up with these do-gooders from hither and yon and their efforts to bring the blessings of their kind of society to us poor benighted Mississippians."[155]

White Alabamians were not unsympathetic to their white neighbors to the west. As news of the Goodman, Schwerner, and Chaney disappearance quickly went national, and as whites in Mississippi loudly, and in unison, proclaimed it a hoax, sightings of the men came rolling into Jackson and beyond. At least one was credible enough to end up on the desks of the governor and the Sovereignty Commission director. Colonel Al Lingo, head of the Alabama Highway Patrol—whose national infamy awaited, nine months hence, on the Edmund Pettus Bridge in Selma—wrote that Andrew Goodman had been spotted in the early evening of June 23 at the Burger-Treat Drive-In at the intersection of Highways 5 and 14 in Marion, Alabama. Witnessed by no fewer than seven employees and patrons, Goodman and three travel companions—including a "very light-skinned" Negro—had their car serviced while dining at the Burger-Treat. At least one of the men had a northern accent, and the group appeared to be headed toward Tuscaloosa.[156]

While some Mississippians clearly remained in denial, there was no denying that the flood of media and FBI agents almost overnight brought something of the shield experienced during the Freedom Vote and the Freedom Day event in Hattiesburg. Certainly, Klan-inspired violence and intimidation were legion as June turned to July. But as Lawrence Guyot would later note, when asked why more people weren't murdered that summer, "The only reason more people weren't killed was because of the timing of the Schwerner, Chaney, and Goodman killings, the involvement of the President in the search, and his denunciation of the act by having the search conducted." Asked a follow-up question about what would have happened to project organizers without the president's intervention, Guyot deadpanned, "You would be conducting this interview with someone else."[157] Similarly, volunteer Elizabeth Martinez noted that the events in Philadelphia, "as much as anything, made the Summer Project less bloody than everyone had expected. And so in some areas, it seemed as though the circling police cars were there to protect the volunteers—at least from being killed."[158] Guyot's and Martinez's accounts about a lack of deaths would be questioned, albeit implicitly, by several colleagues in SNCC many years removed from the events of Freedom Summer.

"... getting fat like a big hog"

Everything changed and nothing changed when Mr. and Mrs. Bowles went fishing on Sunday, July 12. The bound body, wearing Schwerner's signature jeans, sneakers, and a suggestive M belt buckle, sure sounded right. A bound body in a Mississippi river/swamp sounded right, too. How he'd been transported to the other side of the state didn't really matter, nor did details about the fact that the upper half of the body was missing. Surely this was the break the federal government and the press were looking for. Until it wasn't, of course. Had Charles Moore's body been discovered in late May or early June, we would likely not have moving images of its discovery and removal, nor of Dee's. In fact, most likely we wouldn't have any images at all beyond the obligatory coroner postmortems. But because a massive press contingent had settled in for the duration of the search, news of the three civil rights workers' bodies being potentially discovered in the Old River prompted a frenzied response. That response, and the immediate authorization of more divers, seines, and dredging by the FBI's Joseph Sullivan, who was directing the organization's efforts in and around Neshoba County, led to the discovery of Dee's body on July 13. While many would later claim that the FBI discovered Moore's and Dee's bodies while looking for Goodman, Schwerner, and Chaney, that simply wasn't true; rather, the accidental discovery of Moore's corpse by the Bowleses would lead to the discovery of Dee's body the following day.[159]

Both discoveries would reverberate around the state—with vastly different audiences and in very different places.

One of the first men who likely understood the full ramifications of what and who had been discovered in the Old River was Rev. Clyde Briggs. Recall that Rev. Briggs's church in Roxie, Colored Baptist, was the supposed secret location of the Black Muslims' gun-smuggling operation, per Dee and Moore's forced confession in the Homochitto National Forest on May 2. Whether Briggs knew that two teenagers had met their deaths because of the fact that no guns or munitions were found at his church, or if he even knew that Henry Dee and Charles Moore were missing and linked to him, any uncertainty was staunched very quickly. Almost immediately after the bodies had been discovered in the Old River, the Bunkley Klan fired into Briggs's home on July 13. Barely missing his sleeping daughter, Chastity, whose bedroom was on the north side of the house facing the highway, the bullet lodged in a doorframe. The warning shot sent a clear message: talk to the FBI and you and your family are next.[160] Six months later, the intrepid educator and minister was dead—rumored to have been poisoned—at the age of forty-two.

Whether or not James Ford Seale fired the bullet into the Briggs home, the twenty-nine-year-old Klansman was clearly agitated by the discovery of the bodies of Moore and Dee. Not only had he expressed concern to fellow Klansmen that his fingerprints would be on the duct tape used to bind their wrists and seal their mouths, but the FBI's enormous presence in the state after the disappearance of Goodman, Schwerner, and Chaney was being felt, especially in the southwest near Natchez. All of which led Seale to do a curious thing: he wrote a nearly twelve-hundred-word editorial, headed to Meadville, and met Dave Webb at the *Franklin Advocate*, per the paper's policy, and lobbied for its publication. Webb and his copublisher wife, Mary Lou, insisted that all letters to the editor had to be presented in person in order to authenticate the author's prose and vet the content.[161] Seale had a receptive audience: Webb had just been named, very publicly, as state-level director of publicity for the Association for the Preservation of the White Race. Given that the APWR was a front organization for the White Knights, Seale and the Webbs likely knew each other well. And so the newspaper owners needed little persuading: the lengthy editorial ran on Thursday, July 23; it was special enough to receive its own text box and the bold headline, "People Should Fight Communist Menace . . . Obey God's Law First and Foremost."[162]

Seale's anger was directed at any and all elected officials who pledged to abide by the Civil Rights Act of 1964—even if they'd voted against it. Lawmakers who urged constituents to abide by the law's new provisions— signed into law by President Johnson on July 2—weren't just wrong in making such a plea; rather, they were clearly communists intent on subverting the will of God on the race question. "You don't have to listen to your Governor, congressman, senator or a mayor," claimed Seale, "who can turn out to be another Judas or some other snake in the grass, who have been elected by hook and by crook into public office to be called our 'LAW.'" Mixing the Old Testament expulsion from Eden with the Passion of the New, the fevered Klansman pledged allegiance only to God's law. While part of the problem was the inherent corruption of career politicians, Seale colorfully blamed their constituents too: "The reason we have these Judas's [sic] and communist garbage in our public offices is because we have too many so called American Citizens that sit on their big fat lazy bottoms watching a western on T.V. sucking a beer bottle and getting fat like a big hog." Further, the lard-assed, beer-swilling Mississippian wouldn't even watch non-entertainment fare: "And when the news comes on they change channels to get another western or gangster. Most of these so called American people don't even register and vote, when asked to go vote."

James Ford Seale and his family members didn't need a pretext for kidnapping, beating, and murdering, but he attempted to offer one to readers of the *Advocate*: "With the help of God we the people can win this battle by praying, fighting and resisting this bill to the fullest extent of Human ability and at election time by sticking together and voting an unpledged ticket, and kicking all the rotten communist garbage out of our public office." Like the proponents of Massive Resistance following the Supreme Court's

Brown verdict in 1954, a movement championed by senator James O. Eastland, Seale's patriotism was fueled by God, Country, and no doubt Guns to carry out the battle plan against the encroaching communist dictatorship. Straight out of the Sam Bowers playbook for the Klan's countermovement, all of the talk about voting, communists, God, and patriotism was mere pretext; Seale finally reached the racial apotheosis in mid-letter:

> The so called Civil Rights Bill is supposed to help the n----- both North and South. It is supposed to help the n----- get equal schools, when in most places in the south they have better schools. It is supposed to give the n----- equal voting rights, when in the South, if a n----- is qualified to vote, he can, if not he is turned away, the same applies to white people. But the above things are not what they want, they want to eat in the white café, sleep in the white hotel or motel, swim in the white pool, go to the white church, go to the white school, in short, they want to marry your white daughter, or live with her, the only thing they know.

The public accommodations provision of the new Civil Rights Act, any self-respecting Klansman knew, was mere pretext. The Black beast rapist simply couldn't help himself when it came to white women; it was the "only thing" he knew—and could ever know. Seale closed his lengthy epistle with a flurry of rhetorical criticism: the Bible, as the sole valid source of American law, was very clear when it came to racial segregation: separate was equal in God's eyes. From the Old Testament prophets Ezra and Nehemiah to the Law of Moses, God was the original segregationist, a point made repeatedly in many a Southern white pulpit.

It's hardly a surprise that at the very moment when James Ford Seale's future freedom threatened to be clouded by the headless torsos hauled out of the Old River, and with a president and his administration flexing their investigative muscle in Mississippi, the truck driver turned scriptural hermeneut and Strict Constitutional Originalist might find solace in his Bible. Surely patriotic Mississippi men (and women) were right to take up arms against a communist (and thus satanic) plot against America. Even murdering innocent Black teenagers could be rationalized under such circumstances, couldn't it? "Collateral damage" was bound to occur in the coming race war, even as an early grave prevented the inevitable "mingling" engendered by promiscuously enforced desegregation.

Seale's letter to the editor was officially entered into evidence in June 2007; forty-three years on, prosecutors could not have asked for a better character witness than the Klansman himself.

Back in Franklin County, a scorching-hot July came and went. The small weekly newspaper published nary a word about the disappearance and murder of Goodman, Schwerner, and Chaney—except to complain about the ongoing search. "The real purpose of the whole affair," opined the white supremacist Dave Webb, "is to provide an excuse to send federal forces into Mississippi. The whole rotten mess stinks to high heaven."[163] No doubt the rotting corpses of Moore and Dee had gotten into the nostrils of the white Mississippians who'd hoped the bodies would forever remain anchored to the river bottom.

". . . two previously unsuspected slayings"

Yet even as many Mississippi publishers tried to ignore the biggest news story in the United States unfolding in their backyard, the *Franklin Advocate* ran a page 1 story on the discovery of Moore's and Dee's bodies, going so far as to identify the teenagers as "local Negroes." Other important details, though, were erroneous: Moore had not been "expelled" from Alcorn A&M "following a riot on the campus last spring," and the men had not been seeking work with relatives in Albany, Louisiana, contrary to Sheriff Wayne Hutto's account. In fact, Hutto clearly lied to Dave Webb: Moore's and Dee's relatives in Albany had not informed him that the two teenagers were safe in Louisiana; Mazie Moore and Thelma Collins had exploded that lie back in early May. But the short article did end on a truthful note: neither Moore nor Dee was "involved in racial conflicts." The entire Bunkley Klavern knew that, as did its most prominent local member, Sheriff Hutto: Roxie Colored Baptist proved it—Black do-rags notwithstanding.

The *Advocate* wasn't alone in reporting the grisly discovery: from Hattiesburg and Natchez, to Jackson, Vicksburg, and Meridian, and to Greenville, Greenwood, and Clarksdale, the Mississippi press featured the story on their front pages. Of course news of the suspicious death of two Mississippi Negro teenagers was page 1 news around the state only because of the ongoing three-week search for Goodman, Schwerner, and Chaney. Subtract that unfolding blockbuster played out on a national stage and the Moore and Dee discovery becomes, at best, a local, back-page, and un-bylined story.[164] Typical was the lede of the Jackson *Clarion Ledger*: "A second partial body found in a river 17 miles south of here [Tallulah, Louisiana] was not one of the three civil rights workers who vanished in Mississippi, it was reported Monday night."[165] And from the *Hattiesburg American*: "Officials ordered a search of the Old River on the possibility that the body found Sunday might be one of the three civil rights workers who vanished near Philadelphia, Mississippi, June 21."[166] The *Delta Democrat-Times*'s front-page headline read: "College President Identifies Body; CR Trio Ruled Out," even as the United Press International bylined article confidently claimed that the first corpse was that of a white man.[167] And the *Greenwood Commonwealth* made obvious what many journalists (and activists) were thinking: "The search for three missing Mississippi civil rights workers seems to have turned up two previously unsuspected slayings and a new mystery for officers."[168]

Bob Moses and his COFO team might have been pleasantly surprised to see the white Mississippi press scramble to cover the Moore and Dee story; they might have been less surprised, though, by what they read in the *New York Times*. For three long years, SNCC and CORE had labored without media attention in the lonely outposts of Mississippi now attracting the nation's collective gaze—including its president, its top lawyer, and its most important investigative body. Prominent, well-educated white lives mattered. "A fisherman found the lower half of a body," the *Times* story began, "its legs tied together, floating in the Mississippi River today. Authorities rushed it here [Jackson] to determine if it was one of the three civil rights workers who disappeared three weeks ago."[169]

John Herbers authored a follow-up to Monday's UPI story on July 14. Under the words "A 2D BODY IS FOUND IN THE MISSISSIPPI," a secondary headline read, "No Link Seen to 3 Missing Civil Rights Workers." While Herbers reported more specifics about Henry Dee and Charles Moore, the press still couldn't report accurate details on their disappearance: The *Times* claimed that the two men had "been missing since April 25," that "their disappearance had not been reported to authorities," and that "relatives said they assumed the two had gone to Louisiana to find work." No doubt borrowing from stories about Sheriff Hutto's purposefully misleading claims, Herbers did report fears that Dee and Moore "were the victims of another racial killing in Southwest Mississippi, the center of terrorist activities in recent months." He did not elaborate on who the "others" were.

Dee and Moore's final appearance in the *Times* during the summer of 1964 came the following day, July 15, when Herbers reported not from Jackson but on the ground in Meadville and Roxie. Specifically, the *Times*'s lead civil rights reporter talked with Mazie Moore, three of Dee's relatives, and Wayne Hutto. Several corrections to the previous day's story were made: the teenagers disappeared from Meadville near noon on May 2; they'd been reported missing by family members on May 5 to Sheriff Hutto; and relatives had gone looking for the two in Albany, Louisiana, one hundred miles to the south, and found nothing. A close reading of the page 17 story led to only one plausible conclusion: Hutto was lying. "I can't figure it out," the lawman professed. "If these boys had been in any trouble around here, I think I would have known about it."[170] Whether Herbers pressed the prevaricating cop/Klansman that the relatives in Albany never stated that Dee and Moore were safe there, per Hutto's claim, or that he'd even called them, the *Times* had planted doubts about the sheriff's "investigation."

As the presumed murders of Moore and Dee played out across Mississippi and the nation—typically in the context of the search for Goodman, Schwerner, and Chaney—the grisly discovery in the Old River also quickly made its way to the Oval Office. On the morning of July 13, Johnson received a call from FBI director J. Edgar Hoover, who'd just flown back from opening the bureau's new state headquarters in Jackson. That two very high-powered presidential proxies—Dulles and Hoover—had been dispatched to Mississippi in the immediate aftermath of the three civil rights workers' disappearance spoke volumes about presidential priorities and the national importance of the unfolding story. "Edgar," as Johnson referred to Hoover, had important new information: two bodies had been discovered 120 miles away from Neshoba County; no, they were "not connected with the Philadelphia case"; and because both bodies had been bound and drowned, foul play was suspected. Twice during the seven-minute conversation did Hoover say that "it looks as if we've got another [civil rights] case."[171] The director, of course, was well aware of the Klan violence in the southwestern part of the state, and both bodies suggested to him a possible racial motive. Whether the FBI would have even investigated the murders of Moore and Dee without the Neshoba County influence is open to speculation. But the FBI's extensive investigation, directed by

Hoover and approved by the Justice Department, would lead to the arrest of James Ford Seale and Charles Marcus Edwards on November 7, 1964, long after the summer volunteers had gone back to campus and begun their fall semester. And while the Franklin County district attorney refused to prosecute the men on the most spurious of grounds, the FBI's investigation would serve as the cornerstone of Seale's successful prosecution forty-three years later.[172]

Some seasoned COFO veterans weren't terribly fazed by the discoveries of the headless torsos in the Old River; Black bodies being murdered and thrown into Mississippi's swamps and rivers had a long, torturous history. Roy Torkington, a white volunteer from Berkeley, California, assigned to Itta Bena in Leflore County, learned some of that history from locals. In a letter to his fiancée, Anne, Torkington wrote, the Yazoo River "is, as Albert Darner said, 'Dat river where dey floats them bodies in.' The river is the traditional place for dumping a Negro after a lynching." A local Black woman, "Mrs. Williams," had relayed a story to the aghast volunteers: "She was in a rowboat fishing in the Sunflower River when something hit the boat. It was a dead Negro. She rowed the boat away and let the corpse float on." The incredulous volunteers asked the logical and white question: Had she reported it? No, Williams replied, "in those days a dead n----- floatin' in the river was as common as a snake."[173] From the small COFO project in Tchula, in western Holmes County at the eastern border of the Delta, one exasperated volunteer wrote to his parents, "Yesterday while the Mississippi River was being dragged looking for the three missing civil rights workers, two bodies of Negroes were found—one cut in half and one without a head. Mississippi is the only state where you can drag a river any time and find bodies you were not expecting. . . . Negroes disappear down here every week and are never heard about. . . . Jesus Christ, this is supposed to be America in 1964."[174]

" . . . bodies found"

Though expressing a similar sentiment—Black life and death in Mississippi was both cheap and common—note a critical difference: Mrs. Williams referenced a past—"in those days"—whereas the white Tchula volunteer expressed a present (and future?) reality. How far in the past, the Itta Bena resident did not say, but at least some influential voices used the seeming coincidental discovery of Moore's and Dee's mutilated Black bodies as proof that "floating" or submerged bodies were not uncommon. Two of those voices belonged to folk singer Phil Ochs and Marshall "Matt" Jones of the SNCC Freedom Singers, both of whom wrote songs whose inventional impetus can be traced rather directly to the Old River and Parker's Landing. Both songs, but Jones's in particular, would also later serve a useful synecdochic function in dramatizing the deadly events from Freedom Summer. That is, rather than a singular and exceptional instance of racial violence, the discovery of Moore's and Dee's bodies moved in the other direction: the story represented just how common white-on-Black murder was. Ochs's opening stanza of "Here's to the State of Mississippi" proclaimed,

> For underneath her borders, the devil draws no lines
> If you drag her muddy river, nameless bodies you will find
> Whoa the fat trees of the forest have hid a thousand crimes
> The calendar is lyin' when it reads the present time[175]

Ochs's lyrics clearly reference the "Big Muddy," the Mississippi River, rather than a more ubiquitous and plural "rivers," and thus make a more specific reference to Moore and Dee. Interestingly, though, Ochs renders the discovered bodies as both nameless and raceless. But to find a nameless body in the Mississippi River, so the song's logic suggests, was to always already identify its race. That Moore and Dee do not get named in the song, as we will see later, suggests a rather willful historical amnesia that continues to enact the rhetorical logic of the lyrics. In a word, Black bodies pulled out of rivers can't be named if the random and common white terror is to be believed. To name is to specify, to localize, and to make singular.

Matt Jones, who performed around the country as part of SNCC's very popular Freedom Singers, composed "In the Mississippi River" in the aftermath of the discoveries of July 12 and 13. As with Ochs, the song's lyrics feature only that river as the site of racial violence, thereby making allusion to Moore and Dee. The movement of the lyrics is to count the accumulating number of victims, from "one by one" to the final stanza's "ten by ten." Further, the racial victims have "hands tied," "feet tied," and "their heads cut off." Again, the allusions to Moore and Dee are pronounced even as their names are never mentioned. That carefully preserved anonymity, though, is not extended for the white victims; Jones mentions Goodman and Schwerner (and also Chaney) by name.[176] Their status as white and exceptional victims is enshrined with the mention of their names; to be a white victim of racial violence in Mississippi is to specify a history and thus a future.

Similarly, in Tom Paxton's 1964 folk song "Goodman and Schwerner and Chaney," the trio serves as the title and chorus, while Moore and Dee are again rendered nameless. The song's third stanza reads,

> The Pearl River was dragged and two bodies found
> But it was a blind alley because both men were brown

While naval airmen from nearby Meridian did in fact drag the Pearl River in and around Neshoba County on orders from the president, no bodies—white or Black—were discovered there. The historical veracity of where Moore and Dee were eventually discovered matters less than the fact of their brownness, which again renders both men anonymous in death. The stanza continues, "So they all shrugged their shoulders and the search it went on." Whether the "shrug" suggests a callous indifference or something more benign, the blindness of which Paxton sings represents a symbolic field in which signification—naming—is impossible. To be brown is to have no voice and no face—and thus to inhabit the rhetorical void. To be white, on the other hand, or in the company of whites, per James Chaney, is to command notice and legitimacy from both the government and its citizens:

> For they've murdered two white men, and a colored boy too
> Goodman and Schwerner and Chaney.

That Goodman and Schwerner are named as "men" and Chaney is given the diminutive and racially coded "boy" is apposite. While the nation was "shocked," it would "call J. Edgar Hoover. He'll know what to do." The nation and its legendary investigator's reactions are predicated on a wholly determinative skin color. Hoover's knowing protocols and the nation's shock are twinned to whiteness and thus naming.

Though they couldn't have known it, the white volunteers and the singer-songwriters, at this very early hour in Freedom Summer historiography—really before the history writing even began—had set an important rhetorical precedent: Goodman, Schwerner, and Chaney would be enshrined at the very center of the interracial story to bring Mississippi into the nation; Moore and Dee, by contrast, would be infrequently named, their history would often be erroneous, if not altogether forgotten, and their story would be lumped in to a more generalized racial terror that left Black bodies storyless, placeless, nameless, and even limbless.[177] Neither letter-writing nor popular culture can or should bear the burden of a complexly layered history, but even before Freedom Summer had come to a close, some of its discursive landscape was being shaped in particular directions by those closest to it. That landscape also had important antecedents in COFO's rationale for the Summer Project in the first place: white lives mattered to the press and the federal government in ways that those of Black Mississippians simply did not. In brief, the (his)story of what would become Freedom Summer had already been carefully, if unknowingly, cultivated by its principal architects. Of course Andrew Goodman, Mickey Schwerner, and James Chaney would serve as a thematic anchor, but the generic parameters of the story had been written well before the story's particulars unfolded in Neshoba County. Bob Moses had already authored it.

Ella Baker tried to fight back against the rhetorical landscape she could see forming. Much like Rita Schwerner back in late June, the organizational genius behind SNCC tried mightily to locate a rhetorical equivalence for white and Black bodies. SNCC's motto was "Where is your body"—less a question and more of a badge of embodied honor. SNCC'ers proudly bled and sacrificed in the fight for civil rights, and their iconic white-and-Black handshake symbolized that the organization didn't really care if one's body was white or Black. But the country did. And so as the bodies of Goodman, Schwerner, and Chaney were carefully, archaeologically, exhumed at the Old Jolly Farm by the FBI on August 4, forty-four days after they'd exited the Neshoba County Jail into the assembled clutches of the White Knights, a mesmerized nation and world watched. The flimsy body bags, accompanied by the putrid stench of hot decomposing flesh, were unloaded in Jackson for autopsies. Three days later, Baker delivered the keynote address, also in Jackson, at the state convention for the Mississippi Freedom Democratic Party (MFDP). Born in the wake of the Freedom Vote, the MFDP was a parallel political party designed to give Black Mississippians both a (legal) vote and someone to vote for. Soon the sixty-eight delegates would be on their way to Atlantic City, New Jersey, to challenge the seating of the delegation of all-white Mississippi Democrats. The impassioned Baker observed that "the tragedy has become a symbol." The deaths of Goodman, Schwerner, and Chaney had already hardened into rhetorical form and significance. "The unfortunate thing is that it took this kind of symbol to make the rest of the country turn its eyes on the fact that there are other bodies lying under the swamps of Mississippi. Until the killing of a Black mother's son becomes as important as the killing of a white mother's son, we who believe in freedom cannot rest."[178] Whether Baker's optimism was feigned or genuine, whether she was talking about Mazie Moore or Fannie Lee Chaney, the "other [Black] bodies" in the nation's field of vision were quickly on their way to being forgotten; "other" bodies were, by default, Black bodies—and how could a Black body be remembered when it had no name?

It didn't take long for the rapidly calcifying symbolic importance of the three civil rights workers' deaths to achieve near-sacred status. Artist and illustrator Tracy Sugarman published his memoir on Freedom Summer, *Stranger at the Gates*, in 1966. While volunteering in the small community of Ruleville in Sunflower County, Sugarman became close friends with Fannie Lou Hamer, whose unquenchable spirit and oratorical gifts sustained the movement there. She also authored the foreword to Sugarman's memoir. The deeply religious former plantation timekeeper lauded the Freedom Summer volunteers as helping to bring forth God's "New Kingdom right here on earth." Hamer reserved a special place in that Kingdom for the three men murdered by the Klan: "These young people were so Christlike! James Chaney, Andrew Goodman, and Michael Schwerner gave their lives that one day we would be free. If Christ were here today, He would be just like these young people."[179] Hamer's biblically inspired translation of the three men's deaths—now martyrdom—would have its secular equivalents in the nation's collective memory and in Freedom Summer's historiography in the years to come.

". . . there is evidence that people remember things that never happened."

—MICHELLE NORRIS

"...um, nine other bodies"

I first stumbled upon the story of Charles Moore and Henry Dee, by way of Goodman-Schwerner-Chaney, in 2006. As with most beginnings, it took me some time to understand it as such. The originating event, it turns out, was a documentary, *Freedom Summer*, directed by Marco Williams and aired on the History Channel. Not unlike many of its predecessors, the documentary highlighted the disappearance of the three civil rights workers early in the program. In the intervening forty-two years, that event had become The Defining Event of the Summer Project; its importance in collective American memory had been portended before white volunteers had even returned to their campuses. But then a curious thing occurred at the thirty-minute mark of the documentary: grainy black-and-white footage showed what appeared to be law enforcement personnel in small boats in rivers and swamps, obviously looking for Goodman, Schwerner, and Chaney. CORE's Dave Dennis, from the twenty-first century, contextualizes what we are seeing: "During the time that the bodies of Chaney, Schwerner, and Goodman were missing, there were other bodies being found, alright. America did not—the press did not—pick it up. The press did not talk about it." Williams then cuts to professor Gerald Gill, from Tufts University, who further elaborates on Dennis's remarks: "When they were dredging up rivers and creeks in Mississippi, the navy had uncovered numerous other bodies, the bodies of Black men. There was one instance of a Black male torso being discovered wearing a CORE T-shirt. They came up with, um, nine other bodies of, um, unidentified Black males." More on that CORE torso later.

I found Professor Gill's statement shocking, one I'd never encountered before; quickly did I note his name and his university. Dennis then punctuates the segment: "Some of them [Black bodies] were on the side of the road, you know, some of them were in other areas, some were buried; the fact is that they found people, bodies strung up in trees, and things of that nature. And the amazing thing about it was, was that when they discovered that they were not one of the civil rights workers, there was like this sigh of relief."[180] I also noted a rather telling irony after the broadcast: both men refused to name any of the recovered Black bodies, or where the bodies were discovered. Weren't these omissions symptomatic of the larger claims they were both advancing about racial erasure? Why perpetuate the historical claim, good intentions notwithstanding, that such Black bodies *still*—forty-two years later—had no name or place?

I emailed Dr. Gill at his Tufts address the following morning, curious to know more about these "nine other [Black] bodies" found during the search for Goodman, Schwerner, and Chaney. He never wrote back.[181] Whether his silence was a function of an overburdened inbox, an unwillingness to share information, or something else, my curiosity was only galvanized by the stunning claim. If in fact nine other Black bodies were discovered during the forty-four-day search, and if the nation still did not know who they were, by my reckoning, and since I wrote about and taught about the civil rights movement in Mississippi, I was complicit in the conspiracy of silence. Not knowing wasn't an excuse; it was, in fact, precisely part of the larger systemic problem of Black erasure, even as it played out in Freedom Summer historiography. Of course a white rhetorician-historian wouldn't know about it; Goodman, Schwerner, and Chaney occupy nearly all of the discursive-visual-commemorative terrain when it comes to June, July, and August 1964. Ella Baker and Rita Schwerner were still right, four decades on and counting.

With some patient digging, I eventually learned the names Charles Eddie Moore, Henry Hezekiah Dee; I located one or two pictures and I read the details of their deaths. But neither was wearing a CORE T-shirt—and there were only two of them. What of the other seven Black bodies? As any self-respecting Mississippi civil rights historian might do, I consulted John Dittmer's highly esteemed book *Local People: The Struggle for Civil Rights in Mississippi*. Published thirty years after Freedom Summer, and with an entire chapter devoted to the Summer Project, surely this masterful and Bancroft Prize–winning work would clarify the Black bodies question. Dittmer expresses his own historiographical ennui with the Summer Project, titling his Freedom Summer chapter "That Summer"—as if it needed any other designation—and referring to the murders of the three civil rights workers as "depressingly familiar." Dittmer gives only one fleeting and error-filled paragraph to Moore and Dee:

> On July 12, the day after J. Edgar Hoover left Jackson, a fisherman near Tallulah, Louisiana, reported seeing the lower half of a man's body caught on a log in a bayou near the Mississippi River. The next day

the lower half of a second body was discovered nearby. The victims were twenty-year-old Charles Moore, an Alcorn College student, and Henry Dee, twenty-one, neither of whom had been active in the civil rights movement. On May 2, klansmen had abducted the two young men and taken them deep into the Homochitto National Forest, where they bound them to a tree and beat them to death. Their bodies were then tied to an engine block and dumped into the river. . . . The body of a black teenager, never identified, was also found floating in the Big Black River. He was wearing a CORE T-shirt. Once it became clear that these three victims were not the missing COFO workers, the press and the public quickly lost interest.[182]

Leaving aside for the movement the vagaries on key details—near Tallulah, a bayou, a fisherman, Alcorn College rather than A&M, and an engine block—Dittmer gets both men's ages wrong; both Dee and Moore were alive when they were drowned; "the river" is never specified, even as it's assumed to be the Mississippi River (is it a bayou or a river?); and the Klan's crime(s) remains motiveless. Furthermore, the "never identified" Black teenager with the supposed CORE T-shirt was in fact immediately identified; he was fourteen-year-old Herbert Orsby from New Orleans, who'd gone missing from his grandparents' house in Pickens, Mississippi, and who likely drowned in the Big Black River on September 7, nearly two weeks after the close of the Summer Project. And his grandfather, Tobe Hart, knew nothing about a CORE T-shirt.[183] And did the press and the public in fact "quickly los[e] interest" in the Dee and Moore case? The Mississippi press covered the story for the better part of a week, and the FBI investigated the case for nearly four months. The *New York Times*, among others, followed the story well into January 1965, when the district attorney dropped charges against Seale and Edwards. Perhaps most importantly, where are the seven other Black bodies discovered during the search for Goodman, Schwerner, and Chaney? Six, if you count the erstwhile Orsby. Was Freedom Summer "depressingly familiar" because of the numbing repetition of erroneous details? Was it "That Summer" because everybody already knew how it began and ended, and how the racialized narrative arc played out? Or had popular culture emptied out Freedom Summer's significance and nuance?

Because of these errors, Dittmer's account raised more questions than it answered, especially on the vexing body count question. I next consulted perhaps the foremost historical account of the three murders, Cagin and Dray's 1988 book (republished in 2006), *We Are Not Afraid: The Story of Goodman, Schwerner, and Chaney, and the Civil Rights Campaign for Mississippi*. Unlike Dittmer, Cagin and Dray flesh out the Moore and Dee drownings and offer motives for the Klan kidnapping and murder. After telling their story in two fact-packed paragraphs, the authors close the Moore and Dee interlude with a final paragraph: "To the horror and disgust of southern Blacks and movement people, several Black corpses were found in Mississippi by authorities searching for Goodman, Schwerner, and Chaney." Presumably, given the chronology and placement of their account, Cagin and Dray are referring to "Black corpses" in addition to those of Moore and Dee. Questions immediately arise: How many constitute "several," where were these bodies discovered, when, and by whom? Cagin and Dray close the paragraph with a sentence rather similar to Dittmer: "One of the saddest discoveries of the season was the body of a never-identified boy, about fourteen, wearing a CORE T-shirt, which was found floating in the Big Black River."[184] Again, the "season" was over and the "never-identified boy" had a name and a place—even an address. In fact, the *St. Louis Argus* ran a headline spanning the entirety of its front page on September 18, announcing the suspicious drowning; other prominent Black newspapers gave rather extensive space to Herbert Orsby's death.[185] The story calls to mind the death of Emmett Till, another fourteen-year-old boy fished out of a Mississippi river just nine years earlier, so why didn't Cagin and Dray offer even a name—and guess at, rather than confirm, an age? And they had eighteen years to correct the book's first edition. Were nameless Black bodies the order of the historiographical day? Did we need even more Mississippi horror than the dead Black bodies we could count—and name? Why?

I next consulted the highly acclaimed *Ghosts of Mississippi*, Maryanne Vollers's riveting account of the search for justice in the murder of Medgar Evers. Published in 1995, one year after Dittmer's book and seven years after Cagin and Dray's, her book too wades into the murky waters of Freedom Summer. After giving a brief mention to Moore and Dee, she adds to the body count: "Before the end of the summer another body surfaced in the Big Black River. All that remained was the torso of a thirteen- or fourteen-year-old Black boy wearing a CORE T-shirt."[186] One can readily see how the historiography of the two separate cases has merged into a very misleading depiction: Again, Orsby had a fully membered corpse; he had a name; he had a definite age; he was not part of Freedom Summer; and his grandfather said he was not wearing a CORE T-shirt. In brief, the death of Herbert Orsby has been uncritically accepted into a historiography that aggregates Black bodies in an attempt to argue that a racist state and country couldn't be bothered with names and details of horribly mutilated Black boys—a tradition seemingly perpetuated in such careless histories.

"Because people forgot . . ."?

Sensing that I might have stumbled onto something, or at least a curious question, I decided to consult the sources closest in time, and perhaps space, to the events of 1964. First up was William Bradford Huie's *Three Lives for Mississippi*. As he did in the Till murder case, Huie interjected himself into the story of Goodman, Schwerner, and Chaney by offering reward money for information leading to the buried bodies.[187] In a lengthy exposition on Klan intrigue, Mississippi resistance, and detailed re-creation, Huie says not a word about any bodies discovered—Black or white—beyond Goodman, Schwerner, and Chaney.[188] Similarly, one of the very first academic histories of the summer, *Mississippi: The Long Hot Summer* by Stanford University's William McCord, contains no mention of Moore and Dee, and nothing about unidentified Black bodies discovered during the hunt for the three men.[189] Too, a survey of current-events publications such as the *Times*, *Time*, and *U.S. News and World Report*, among others, revealed nothing about unnamed Black bodies discovered in June, July, or August. Perhaps most revealing, there is nothing in the monastically documented "Running Summary of Incident Reports" kept by COFO during the summer that even suggests unnamed Black bodies—though scrupulously offering hour-by-hour activity in the early days of the Goodman, Schwerner, and Chaney disappearance.[190] In a 1964 issue of *Ramparts* magazine, titled "Mississippi Eyewitness: The Three Civil Rights Workers—How They Were Murdered," which devoted lengthy articles to the search for the missing men, Moore, Dee, Orsby, and a white carnival worker's body discovered near Oakland, Mississippi, are noted—but no unnamed Black bodies are mentioned.[191]

Revealing, too, are the memoirs published by Mississippi movement veterans, especially those proximate to Freedom Summer. Tracy Sugarman's

1966 memoir of Freedom Summer is silent on Black bodies. The movement's appointed "historian" of Freedom Summer, lawyer Len Holt, also has nothing to say about the discovery of Black bodies during the forty-four-day search for Goodman, Schwerner, and Chaney, nor do any of the letters published in Elizabeth Sutherland-Martinez's anthology.[192] Don Whitehead, who had a very close working relationship with the FBI, says nothing about unidentified Black bodies discovered during the unprecedented search in his 1970 history of the Klan in Mississippi.[193] A bit farther removed in time, James Farmer, for example, who was the executive director of CORE, and who was one of the very first movement personnel to ask face-to-face questions of Cecil Price and Lawrence Rainey, has nothing to say about the discovery of unnamed Black bodies, nor do Stokely Carmichael or Cleveland Sellers—both of whom walked the rivers and swamps searching for their colleagues.[194] Unita Blackwell, a Black SNCC organizer from the tiny Delta community of Mayersville, noted in her memoir that "only" three Black bodies were discovered that summer.[195] One of the most interesting memoirs of the Summer Project, originally published in 1965, by Sally Belfrage, also made no claims about dead Black bodies—until her memoir was reissued in 1990 by the University of Virginia Press. In her preface to that addition, Belfrage, excoriating Hollywood's heroicizing of the FBI in the film *Mississippi Burning*, describes "dragging the rivers and swamps without somehow turning up any of the nameless Black bodies in fact found at the time."[196] In the span of twenty-five years, it appears, nameless Black bodies were discovered and noted.

In searching for early accounts of unnamed Black bodies discovered in the summer search, I frequently wondered what the laconic Bob Moses had to say. I was disappointed that his book, *Radical Equations*, contained few answers. Given that Moses not only was the architect of the Summer Project but also occupies a central place in the rhetorical trajectory of interracial violence anticipating the Project, surely he would have said something about nameless and unidentified Black bodies being discovered. Surely the organizer who leveraged Black invisibility and thus disposability as the principal reason for Freedom Summer in the first place would have noted such a discovery; it would be proof, after all, of much of what he'd been saying since at least November 1963. A colleague pointed me to a 1965 talk Moses delivered at a reunion celebrating the five-year anniversary of SNCC. Reflecting on the ongoing killing in Mississippi, Moses stated, "At the same time that everyone knows about the three [Goodman, Schwerner, and Chaney] who were killed and the people who are on trial for that, no one asks about the two Negro boys [Moore and Dee] whose bodies were severed in half, who were found while they were looking for the other three, because nobody knows about them." Furthermore, "nobody asks why did that grand jury let those people off who were indicted for that crime, on the same day that they indicted the people who were supposed to have killed the other three. And nobody asks because, again, nobody knows about it."[197] While Moses might be forgiven for the erroneous claim that a grand jury was convened in 1964 or 1965 in the Moore and Dee case, he does not, just months after the Summer Project, mention Black bodies beyond Moore and Dee. Nor does he lump the body of Herbert Orsby into the unknown. Moses also didn't see fit to state the obvious: racial knowing, and therefore importance, was premised on the skin color of the victims. More than fifty years after Moses offered his brief remarks, historiography devoted to Freedom Summer continues to bear him out, a point to which I will return.

In my quest to answer the missing Black bodies question, perhaps I was going about things all wrong. Perhaps the reason I wasn't reading about them was because the official sources hadn't gotten around to recording the deaths—not even COFO. While such reasoning seemed admittedly far-fetched, I had nothing to lose in pursuing the possibility with movement veterans whom I had gotten to know through the years. Why not ask the men and women who were on the ground? Perhaps they knew things that official histories simply did not record. And so I first turned to my friend Lawrence Guyot, whose prodigious memory and archive always proved useful and insightful. No, the retired SNCC'er and MFDP chairman exclaimed—and Guyot almost always exclaimed—no unnamed Black bodies were discovered that summer. He was quite sure of it. I next turned to Rev. Edwin King, a friend and a constant benefactor to my students, the would-be white lieutenant governor on the Freedom Ticket in 1963. No— he'd checked his detailed files and his many living sources—they hadn't discovered any such bodies during the Summer Project; he was almost positive. With some trepidation, I next reached out to Mickey Schwerner's widow, Rita (now Rita Bender), who had been most gracious in reliving some of the traumatic days of 1964 with me years earlier via email. She replied promptly; no, she knew of no such bodies either, but encouraged me to reach out to several others who might know. One of those was *Clarion*

Ledger journalist Jerry Mitchell, whose reporting on the Klan, including on James Ford Seale, had helped put several men behind bars, and whose research was legendary. Mitchell confessed that, even as he'd encountered such rumors, too, he didn't know of any sources or any proof that such bodies were ever discovered.

*EYES/NESHOBA/*FREEDOM SUMMER*/*1964

And yet the five bodies claim wouldn't go away; in fact, it seemed only to proliferate, especially as the years rolled on, even among some movement veterans, filmmakers, and civil rights historians. I next turned to the now-iconic documentary *Eyes on the Prize*. Created by Henry Hampton, expertly narrated by SNCC'er Julian Bond, and first aired on television in 1987, this massively ambitious documentary project, now housed at Washington University and available online, might provide answers. So influential was the project that, as several have noted, it solidified the periodization of civil rights history. Beginning with *Brown*, moving to the Emmett Till case, then to the Montgomery Bus Boycott, Hampton and his team provided a tidy time line of civil rights history, the critical places, and the men and women central to it. From Montgomery we move to the student sit-ins, the Freedom Rides, the integration of Ole Miss by James Meredith, the Birmingham campaign, and of course the Pettus Bridge and the movement for voting rights in Selma. Perhaps not surprisingly, Freedom Summer gets its own lengthy segment; Bob Moses and Dave Dennis both figure prominently, as might be expected—to say nothing of white, unnamed college students headed from Oxford, Ohio, to Mississippi. Archival footage from the summer is featured, including several clips of navy personnel searching for Goodman, Schwerner, and Chaney, whose disappearance provides the thematic anchor for the segment. No mention is made of the discovery of unnamed Black bodies. Neither is the discovery of the bodies of Charles Moore and Henry Dee noted.

Those omissions might not appear terribly unusual, but a deeper investigation reveals an important editorial decision; that is, the oral history archive for the project contains all of the interviews with the film's many participants. The Dave Dennis interview, in particular, contains important information that was excised from the documentary's final cut. Specifically,

asked to elaborate on the racial difference of the Summer Project volunteers, and what rhetorical difference that would make, Dennis observed:

> I don't think that a lot of people understood the dangers until this, event
> occurred. See, to give an example of what I'm talking about the differ-
> ence for the, uh, what the summer project brought about, the attention,
> if you recall during the time they were looking for the bodies of uh
> Chaney, Schwerner and Goodman, they found other bodies throughout
> this state. Uh, they found torsos in the Mississippi River, they found
> people who were buried, they even found a few bodies of people on
> the side of roads, and things of that nature. All the time, is the press
> and people saying is, is that we, they had found a body, or they found
> two bodies, the autopsies are being run or whatever you have to see
> whether or not they could be identified as some of the, the three miss-
> ing workers. As soon as it was determined that they were not the three
> workers, or one of the three workers, then everybody said "well, it was
> not the three workers, they're still missing," and those deaths were for-
> gotten, they was looking for the three people. And that's what we were
> talking about in terms of what the freedom uh, summer was all about in
> terms of why it was necessary to bring that attention on. Because people
> forgot, and if it had just been Blacks there, we would have forgotten
> again if it had just been three Black people missing. Because what oc-
> curred there is a proof of that is, that the bodies that they found during
> the interval of the first missing of the three workers, in the time that
> they found, there was no real attention given to those deaths.[198]

Dennis's somewhat rambling answer functions as proof that white volunteers were needed precisely because Black lives were valued far less
by the nation, by the press, and by the federal government. Furthermore,
even as Dennis alludes to the bodies of Moore and Dee without naming
them—"torsos in the Mississippi River"—more Black bodies were discovered, bodies that were then quickly "forgotten" as the hunt for Goodman,
Schwerner, and Chaney resumed.

Editors for *Eyes on the Prize* did not run any part of Dave Dennis's
blockbuster claims about the discovery of Black bodies during the search
for the missing three civil rights workers. During the thirty-six-minute
segment on Freedom Summer, a great deal of which is taken up with

the disappearance, discovery, and funerals of Goodman, Schwerner, and Chaney, the film makes no mention of COFO's strategic rhetorical calculus of white-on-white violence; the critically important Freedom Vote is not even referred to, let alone developed; and viewers are left to believe that only three significant murders happened that summer. The only hint that editors even flirted with the idea of including Dennis's claims is a titillating several seconds in which Marshall Jones's "In the Mississippi River" plays over black-and-white moving images filmed at James Chaney's funeral held in Meridian on August 7. The haunting wails of the song cut out at "count them four by four," perhaps a very subtle reference that only four bodies were discovered that summer—and the three that really mattered had just been narratively represented. Dennis's "forgotten" Black bodies remained just that in the civil rights documentary that would largely define the movement for a generation (and beyond?).[199]

The discrepancy I'd unearthed between the archived oral histories and the final film version of *Eyes on the Prize* did nothing to clarify the historical veracity of the missing Black bodies claim; in fact, it only seemed to compound the vexations. Why silence Dave Dennis, COFO's number-two organizer on the ground in Mississippi, on this particular question? Why feature only Goodman, Schwerner, and Chaney when visual evidence could powerfully document the discoveries of Moore's and Dee's corpses? Was Henry Hampton taking sides in this dispute? And if so, was he claiming that white lives still mattered more in 1987 than 1964?

Nearly twenty-fives year later, filmmakers Micki Dickoff and Tony Pagano offered a rather direct retort to the silences of *Eyes on the Prize*. In their award-winning and critically acclaimed 2010 film, *Neshoba: The Price of Freedom*, they chronicle the quest for justice in the murders of the three civil rights workers. That is, while seven men eventually served jail time for their roles in the conspiracy to commit murder, the mastermind of the operation, Baptist preacher and sawyer Edgar Ray Killen, had never been convicted for his role in the murders. At his trial in 1966, jurors voted eleven to one to convict, but a lone holdout claimed that she simply couldn't and wouldn't convict a preacher. As his (re)trial approached, Killen granted the filmmakers unprecedented access to his family, his home, and ultimately himself. But in telling the story of Goodman, Schwerner, and Chaney to a new generation of viewers, Dickoff and Pagano revisited some of the claims made by Dave Dennis. And this time Dennis is accompanied by a new witness: fellow Freedom Summer organizer and Mississippi activist Hollis Watkins. Unlike Dennis, Watkins had been outspokenly against the Summer Project—and remains so—on the grounds that it would undermine the fragile coalition-building that SNCC had been successfully doing with Blacks in the Delta for more than two years. As many of his colleagues argued, a huge influx of educated whites would unalterably affect the racial landscape—organizationally and otherwise.

Dickoff and Pagano tell the story of Goodman, Schwerner, and Chaney's deaths early in their film using a mix of archival footage, present-day interviews, still images, and, of course, music. Early in the film, a much older Rita Schwerner foregrounds the importance of race to the case: "This case has gotten the attention it has gotten because two of the three men were white." Archival footage of James Chaney's mother, Fannie Lou Chaney, follows: "It is no secret . . . if it hadn't been for Mickey Schwerner and Andrew Goodman, my son wouldn't have been known and wouldn't have been found." Whereas Hampton's *Eyes on the Prize* tried to de-emphasize race in its Freedom Summer segment, Dickoff and Pagano highlight it. Following interviews with Jerry Mitchell and Chaney's brother, Ben, the film cuts to black-and-white moving images from the Old River, most likely from July 13, when Henry Dee's body was removed from the water. The FBI's man in charge of the "Miburn" case, a cigar-smoking Joe Sullivan, pulls parts of a body in a bag to a muddy and uneven shore and later handles what appears to be a femur. We hear a poorly edited Dave Dennis talk about the discovery of "two bodies"—again, never named as Henry Dee and Charles Moore—and "everybody holding their breath, hoping that it's not them." We next cut to more archival moving images of the Old River and body bags, then Jones's "In the Mississippi River" cues the next interview. Hollis Watkins states, "As a result of their dragging the Mississippi River, nine additional bodies other than the three civil rights workers were pulled out of the Mississippi River." After dropping this enormous claim, Watkins concludes the segment with a question: "Who are these nine people?" No contextual clues are offered for what we are watching, and whose horribly decomposed bodies are presumably coming out of the Mississippi River. Given the paucity of information, we're led to assume that these bodies belong to some of the nameless "nine people," and that those people, per Rita Schwerner Bender and Fannie Lee Chaney's earlier remarks, are Black. Part of Watkins's explosive claim is just dead wrong:

no bodies—Black or white—came out of the Mississippi River during the search for the three men.

But Watkins's question—"Who are these nine bodies?"—along with the gruesome images of bones and bags, haunts this brief interlude. While his query functions as a rhetorical question and thus no attempt at an answer is made, other questions come to the surface: Don't the filmmakers have an ethical obligation to at least identify the remains of what's coming out of the Old River? Because the filmmakers leave Henry Dee and Charles Moore nameless in death—when they could very easily identify them—the claim of nameless Black bodies continues in perpetuity—as does the suppressed premise: Black bodies, regardless of the number, don't really matter. Then or now. Moreover, why didn't the filmmakers at least pose a challenge to the question in the first place? After all, many movement veterans dispute the claim that nameless Black bodies were discovered—including Rita Schwerner Bender.

The Dickoff and Pagano documentary ends on a note of karmic justice: forty-one years to the day that Goodman, Schwerner, and Chaney were murdered—June 21—Edgar Ray Killen is convicted on three counts of manslaughter and later sentenced to three twenty-year terms, to be served consecutively. In a word, the mastermind of the Klan conspiracy would spend the rest of his life in jail. While many were pleased at the conviction and sentence, others noted a grim fact: of the twenty-one Klansmen involved in the executions, still none had been convicted of murder—whatever the degree. And while Killen's guilt functioned as a sort of collective guilt, we might remember that the Baptist preacher wasn't even at the kidnapping and murder sites on June 21. Moreover, Alton Wayne Roberts, who'd personally pumped bullets into each of the three men, served only six years in federal prison for denying the men their civil rights and would never be tried for the murders he'd directly participated in.

That date, June 21, had been important to the parishioners at Mt. Zion Methodist Church from the murderous night onward; every year the church holds memorial services for the slain men. As the fiftieth anniversary approached, news of yet another documentary was forthcoming: the acclaimed filmmaker Stanley Nelson was writing, directing, and producing a two-hour documentary for PBS's *American Experience*; it promised to be the definitive statement about Freedom Summer. With no small media fanfare, the film aired around the country in June of 2014. The program and its many interviews and resources are now hosted at the PBS.org website. Of course I was very keen to see how Nelson handled the unnamed Black bodies claim. Would he give the Dennis and Watkins claims a hearing, a brief gloss, or a calculated silence?

None of the above, as it turned out. Neither does Nelson say a word about the originating event of the Summer Project, the Freedom Vote of 1963, nor the crucible of race, publicity, and the promise of federal protection it engendered; instead, comedian Dick Gregory's airlift of food to the Delta in January of 1963 is identified as the originating event for Freedom Summer—a completely groundless claim.[200] To Nelson's credit, though, Goodman, Schwerner, and Chaney do not dominate the narrative arc of the film, and viewers also get a relatively fresh cast of Summer Project characters—a mix of volunteers, organizers, and local Mississippians, as well as archival documents that give rich texture to the film, the project's aims, and its many participants. Interestingly, Charles Moore and Henry Dee are never mentioned, nor is archival footage of their recovered bodies shown or discussed. Dave Dennis and Hollis Watkins are both featured in the film, but neither makes mention of the discovery of unnamed Black bodies. In brief, Nelson seems to have editorialized on their sensational claim through the film's silences.

Just when I thought I knew where Nelson stood on the vexing question, I happened across the PBS website supporting the film. Under the tab "General Article: Murder in Mississippi," an unattributed article states, "Throughout July, investigators combed the woods, fields, swamps, and rivers of Mississippi, ultimately finding the remains of eight African American men. Two were identified as Henry Dee and Charles Moore, college students who had been kidnapped, beaten, and murdered in May 1964. Another corpse was wearing a CORE t-shirt. Even less information was recorded about the five other bodies discovered."[201] This important addenda to the film reprises much that we've already encountered—most notably "the five other [Black] bodies." But we also know that Henry Dee wasn't a college student and the supposed CORE-wearing corpse in question belonged to fourteen-year-old Herbert Orsby; we also know where and when and how his body was recovered—and that his body was definitely not found in July. Whether the still-active article is the manifestation of a passive-aggressive filmmaker unwilling to assert on film what someone (erroneously) claims supplementally online or something else, these additional resources, under the PBS imprimatur, do nothing to resolve the matter. In fact, by raising the issue in a strictly discursive and unattributed context, and far from the finished text of the documentary, Nelson and PBS have only confused the matter further. A careful reader might also wonder, By whom, where, and why were Moore and Dee "kidnapped, beaten, and murdered"? By hyperbolizing such violence without any context, the article gives readers a skewed and erroneous representation of what supposedly happened during Freedom Summer. One also wonders, somewhat morosely, about the sad ironies of the final sentence: all anybody apparently "knows," with no corroborating evidence, is that six Black bodies not named Moore, Dee, and Orsby were discovered that July. "Even less information" functions rhetorically as a not-so-subtly coded racial indictment—but against whom? The enthymematic conclusion is simply that "even less information" is known because Black lives in July of 1964 didn't matter enough to unearth it—even as the Moore, Dee, and Orsby cases give the lie to such a conclusion. That we have "even less information" is not a compelling warrant for making such an explosive, race-based claim; if anything, it should function in just the opposite manner. Until we have such information, might we err on the historiographical side of caution?

Curiously, that is exactly what another PBS *American Experience* documentary did in 2014. Stephen Ives's very engaging film *1964* offers a commemorative take on this touchstone year.[202] Viewers are treated to cultural icons such as the Beatles and sporting celebrities such as Cassius Clay/Muhammad Ali. Civil rights is captured in a lengthy segment, not on Dr. King and the Southern Christian Leadership Conference's ongoing desegregation campaign in St. Augustine, Florida, but on Freedom Summer. Predictably, the search for Goodman, Schwerner, and Chaney dominates the narrative. Interviews with Bob Moses, Rita Schwerner Bender, Ed King, and Dave Dennis are again featured. No mention is made of Charles Moore, Henry Dee, or Herbert Orsby, nor is archival footage included from the Old River. But Ives does allow Dennis to state, "They were finding bodies in Mississippi, while they were looking [for Goodman, Schwerner, and Chaney] they were finding bodies . . . you're finding bodies, but they were Black bodies." In brief, Ives's editing strategically omits a number and other specifics, but allows the more general claim to be made: namely, that white lives mattered in far more compelling ways in 1964.

"I only learned later..."

But as the fiftieth anniversary of Freedom Summer was celebrated, the claim that nine, eight, or five nameless Black bodies were discovered during the search for the missing civil rights workers seemed to have become legion among journalists, a taken-for-granted fact of Mississippi terrorism. In an article for *Colorlines*, for example, Carla Murphy quotes summer volunteer Heather Tobis Booth, then eighteen years old: "I was frightened all the time. I was insecure. I think lots of young women especially are. I was afraid that I didn't know enough, that I might harm someone else with my actions. I was also frightened for my life. But I realized that poor Black people in Mississippi lived with that kind of terror every day. I only learned later that while looking for the three missing young men, they found the bodies of eight other Black men. Their hands were bound. Their feet had been chopped off. They'd been thrown into the Mississippi River and those murders had never even been reported."[203] One can glimpse the unsourced claim growing: we now have different maimed body parts, no names at all, and all the bodies were discovered during the search for Goodman, Schwerner, and Chaney.

Mary King, a COFO/SNCC staffer who ran the communications office in Jackson, and who led the efforts to locate the three men immediately after they had failed to report back to Meridian, notes, "When efforts began to dredge the Pearl, Tallahatchie and other rivers to find the bodies, many other corpses were found, frequently with their hands tied behind their backs."[204] King doesn't name any of the "many" bodies, nor was the Tallahatchie River dredged that summer, and the recovered remains of Moore and Dee had no arms or hands. In his fiftieth anniversary article, journalist Askia Muhammad claimed, "Ironically, in the desperate search before those three bodies were found in an earthen grave in Neshoba County, authorities dredged many lakes and ponds. They found body after body, after body of Black men who had previously disappeared without any public outcry."[205] Even as the claim is unsourced, one can sense an increase in the body count, and we are moved well beyond Black bodies in just the Mississippi River.

In the *Tri-State Defender*, George E. Curry claimed that "while looking for the three civil rights workers in rivers and swamps, other Black bodies were discovered. One was Herbert Oarsby [*sic*], a 14-year-old boy who was wearing a Congress of Racial Equality (CORE) T-shirt. The bodies of Henry Hezekiah Dee and Charles Eddie Moore, who had been expelled from Alcorn A&M College for civil rights activities, were also discovered. The remains of five more Black men were found, but never identified."[206] Orsby, of course, wasn't found dead during the search for Goodman, Schwerner, and Chaney; Dee never attended Alcorn A&M College; Moore had not been expelled from said college; and Moore had never engaged in civil rights activity. In Nikole Hannah-Jones's anniversary piece for *The Atlantic*, she claims, "The federal government swarmed Mississippi. The FBI opened an office there for the first time in two decades. The nation's eyes wound up riveted on a place that many felt had existed outside the laws of the land. And as law enforcement dragged rivers searching for the missing civil-rights workers, they found at least nine bodies of Black men who'd disappeared well before."[207] Why Hannah-Jones includes the modifier "at least" is not specified, though it strongly suggests that more unidentified Black bodies were discovered that summer.

Chuck McDew, one of the founders of SNCC and a chairman of the organization, like Dave Dennis, was an early proponent of the "many nameless Black bodies" theory of Freedom Summer. In a 1993 interview, for example, Rosalind Bentley's newspaper article begins dramatically, "Charles (Chuck) McDew watched in disbelief as the beheaded body of a young civil rights worker was pulled from a Mississippi riverbed during the summer of 1964. 'Freedom Now,' read the T-shirt clinging to the boy's battered body." A hybrid racial bouillabaisse, this account borrows from both the Moore and Dee discovery as well as vestiges of the Orsby discovery. It continues: As officials searched for Goodman, Schwerner, and Chaney, "paralyzing anger overwhelmed McDew as body after body of nameless Black men were pulled from the Natchez and Pearl rivers. None of them were the three workers officials were searching for."[208] Not only did at least two of the Black bodies have a name—Orsby's body wasn't discovered until a month after the discovery of the three missing civil rights workers—but a Natchez River doesn't exist, nor were any bodies discovered in the Pearl. Further, the enthymeme is rather explicit: the search for white bodies not only turned up the Black bodies, but said Black bodies were, prima facie, unimportant and thus unnamed.

CORE's Dave Dennis—beginning with an oral history in 1977 and continuing to the present day—claims that five unidentified Black bodies were discovered during the search for the three missing men. In a fiftieth anniversary article for the *Jackson Advocate*, for example, Dennis claimed that even as the Klan had killed Dee, Moore, and Orsby, "the unidentified bodies of five Black men were pulled from Mississippi rivers, the cause unknown."[209] While he lumps Orsby's mysterious death into the Klan's actions against Moore and Dee, Dennis has also slightly modified his earlier claims that nameless Black bodies were being discovered in places well beyond rivers.

Booth, King, McDew, and Dennis were not the only Freedom Summer volunteers and COFO veterans who promulgated the claim that many unidentified Black bodies were discovered during the search for the three missing civil rights workers. Prior to the fiftieth anniversary and the nearly yearlong celebration of the Summer Project, the claim had been made by several participants. Jim Dann, for example, who served with Charles McLaurin and Fannie Lou Hamer in Ruleville and Sunflower County, offered several new and unsourced details: "Although the Navy didn't find the missing trio, what they found was shocking enough. They found bodies of eight Black men probably previously murdered by Rainey and his cronies in the Klan, although this was never proved nor even investigated. . . . Three of them were Black civil rights workers; the other five were never identified. Forty days later, using what today would be called enhanced interrogation techniques, contractors for the FBI finally forced a highway patrolman to reveal where the bodies were buried and name the other killers."[210] Dann's "enhanced interrogation" claim is straight out of the 1988 film *Mississippi Burning* and the infrequently sourced William Bradford Huie account in *Three Lives for Mississippi*. Note, too, that Dann's claim moves the number of bodies to eleven, eight of whom are identified as Black; presumably Moore and Dee and Orsby are civil rights workers; and Rainey's Klan conspiracy is responsible for their deaths. By some credible accounts, most notably one by Jerry Mitchell, the highway patrolman in question is Maynard King, who was not tortured but perhaps paid off handsomely for his confession to FBI lead investigator Joseph Sullivan.[211]

John Lewis, then chairman of SNCC, and veteran of countless arrests and beatings, who had represented the militant arm of the movement at the March on Washington, featured Freedom Summer in his best-selling memoir, *Walking with the Wind*. "Rivers were dragged, woods were scoured, dirt was turned . . . and bodies were found. Old bodies, unidentified corpses, the decomposed remains of Black people long given up as 'missing.' ... One torso, that of a young teenaged boy, was clad in an old CORE T-shirt. It was ugly, sickening, horrifying. Here was proof—as if it was needed—that those woods and rivers in the heart of the Delta had long been a killing field, a dumping ground for the Klan." Note how Lewis, like many before him, erroneously mixes the Moore and Dee and Orsby deaths. The "young teenaged boy," now wearing an "old CORE T-shirt" and survived only by a torso, is likely the fourteen-year-old discovered in the Big Black River near Pickens in September. That he has no name, nor a full body, badly mischaracterizes his story. While Lewis doesn't offer a number, it's clear that the search for Goodman, Schwerner, and Chaney had unearthed many—countless?—Black bodies. Lewis's "proof" turns out to be a poor accounting of what occurred, where it occurred, and what was found during that forty-four-day search. That Moore, Dee, and Orsby are unnamed in Lewis's memoir continues a troubling historiographic trend.

Interviewed for the Proctor Oral History Project at the University of Florida, Allen Cooper, a white volunteer from New Mexico who was assigned to the Sunflower County seat in Indianola, stated, "When they were looking for Chaney, Schwerner and Goodman, they found the bodies of six other, six Black men, who had been tortured and killed. By accident, they found them, with grappling hooks. Just checking swamps, rivers, lakes, streams, whatever, they found bodies." Furthermore, "they didn't do a goddamn thing to look, to find out who they were, how they died, no investigation. The only one they investigated was Chaney, Schwerner and Goodman; it's because Schwerner and Goodman were white. You already know all that shit."[212] The white Cooper lays bare the racial logic advanced by so many following the summer: white lives mattered in far different and more valued ways than Black ones. But Cooper's claim participates, again, in the same historiographic trend: Black bodies get no name, and because they have no name they can have no history. Cooper, like so many, hasn't done "a goddamn thing" to figure out who these Black victims were or try to tell their stories. Black lives don't matter in absentia—and in perpetuity.

Unlike Booth, King, Dann, Lewis, and Allen, photographer and SNCC employee Matt Herron, who formed the Southern Documentary Project for the summer of 1964 in Mississippi, offered more-specific information on the unidentified Black bodies claim. "Black people went missing all the time, and occasionally whites. When FBI agents dragged the

Yockanookany River in the summer of 1964 for the bodies of murdered Civil Rights workers, they didn't find Mickey Schwerner, James Chaney, or Andrew Goodman, but they did find the bodies of nearly a dozen anonymous Black men, some weighted down with chains and bearing marks of torture."[213] I confess that, upon reading Herron's claim, I had no idea if a Yockanookany River even existed—in Mississippi or elsewhere. But in fact, the Yockanookany, a Choctaw name, flows south and west nearly eighty miles, from just west of Ackerman to east of Canton, where it joins the Pearl River. Forty miles north and west of Philadelphia, the river never touches Neshoba County, nor was it likely searched by law enforcement, the navy, or the FBI. Herron's sui generis claim borders on the fantastical: how that particular out-of-the-way river played such a prominent role in the search for Goodman, Schwerner, and Chaney is without explanation—by Herron or anyone else for that matter. But regardless of the geographic specifics, Herron's unsourced claim is fairly close kin with others who have preceded him: nameless Black bodies—now "nearly a dozen," and some perhaps tortured—were discovered during the forty-four-day search. Moore and Dee can only be vaguely glimpsed in Herron's account, Orsby not at all.

One of the most recent and sensational accounts of the missing Black bodies narrative was offered up by SNCC veteran Hollis Watkins in his memoir, *Brother Hollis: The Sankofa of a Movement Man*.[214] Recall that Watkins was one of the first movement veterans to claim that several unidentified Black bodies were discovered during the search for Goodman, Schwerner, and Chaney. By 2016, though, his claims had gotten a good deal more specific—and far more sinister. He states,

> To add insult to injury, even though the three workers went missing in the Eastern part of the county, law enforcement began dragging the river for bodies in the Western part of the county. In their attempt to make a mockery of the murders and our inability to do anything about the murders, it seemed that God Almighty caused their efforts to prove just how evil they were and just what type of hellish terrorism Black folks endured in Mississippi. While the initial searches did not produce Chaney, Goodman, and Schwerner, they did find multiple Black bodies that had been murdered and stashed in the river. They exhumed so many Black bodies that they were forced by their embarrassment to reveal where the bodies of Chaney, Goodman, and Schwerner lay as a

way to detract from the shock of the number of bodies that had been pulled from the river that most of America was just realizing existed.[215]

Instead of "just" finding Black bodies, Watkins exposes law enforcement's conspiracy to try to conceal the extent of the genocide. This is the first and only time I've read about a conspiracy to distract the nation from unspecified law enforcement's blockbuster discovery of so many Black bodies. It must have been an enormous number of lynched Black bodies for law enforcement to at long last reveal exactly where Goodman, Schwerner, and Chaney were buried. Only a story that massive had the potential to distract the press.

Not only is Watkins's conspiracy theory unsourced, it is also riddled with problems and errors. First, the three men went missing in the far southeastern part of the county—but nobody knew this in June 1964 save for the murderers. The last sighting of the three men alive occurred at the Neshoba County Jail, smack in the middle of the county. In addition, the navy was initially ordered into the area by President Johnson to search the northeast part of Neshoba County near Bogue Chitto, where the burned-out station wagon was discovered on June 23. It only makes sense to search for bodies proximate to where the station wagon was discovered. The navy did not initially search in the western part of Neshoba County. Too, note that "they" and "their" remain unspecified in Watkins's account: we simply don't know who's doing the finding and searching, and most importantly, who's orchestrating the diabolical conspiracy. Moving from 1964 to the present, note that Watkins's prose is also trained on a different group: just as the nation's press was distracted from the really urgent story, so, too, have civil rights historians been misled by law enforcement's conspiracy; after all, we're still writing a good deal about Goodman, Schwerner, and Chaney instead of the "hellish terrorism" endured by Black Mississippians.

If there is an "official word" from the activist community on the unidentified Black bodies question, the contribution of Civil Rights Movement Archive website would qualify. The self-proclaimed cyber headquarters of the "Southern Freedom Movement," hosted by Tougaloo College in Jackson, crmvet.org is an online repository for all manner of oral and written history about the movement, as well as archival materials and present-day contact information. Its lengthy "Mississippi Freedom Summer Events" section features material on the "Lynching of Chaney, Schwerner & Goodman."

Chronicling the search for the missing men, the unattributed article notes that "throwing corpses of murdered Blacks into the nearest river is a traditional component of the 'southern way of life,' so hundreds of Navy sailors are assigned to search the swamps, and Navy divers drag the rivers. Soon Black bodies are being pulled from the waters." The author(s) proceeds to specifics: "Among them are Henry Hezekiah Dee and Charles Eddie Moore, lynched by the Klan after Moore is expelled from Alcorn A&M for participating in civil rights protests. The Klansmen falsely believe that Dee and Moore are 'Black militants' collecting guns for a race war against whites. For this imaginary crime they are murdered." The characterization of Moore's actions is erroneous, and more than two Black bodies are implied with the words "among them," but the history being recounted isn't out of the ordinary. It continues, "Another young victim, tentatively identified as 14-year old Herbert Oarsby [sic], is found wearing a CORE T-shirt. The remains of five other Black men are never identified. But none of the bodies are those of the missing white men, and both the media and the FBI quickly loose [sic] interest in them."[216] Crmvet.org has also lost interest: the five Black men and their histories remain in the void. As I have also documented, the FBI, the national news media, and the state's newspapers did not lose interest, especially concerning the murders of Moore and Dee. Without the FBI's dutiful vigilance, James Ford Seale would never have been prosecuted for their kidnap, beating, and murders; Franklin County sheriff Wayne Hutto was certainly not going to seek evidence or pursue indictments against a fellow Klansman, especially since he was in on the conspiracy.

However, crmvet.org does not speak with one voice on this or any other civil rights matter. Many movement veterans aren't "on" the site. And many movement veterans, as I have noted, are skeptical, if not downright hostile, to the claim that unidentified Black bodies were discovered during the summer of 1964. Project director Bob Moses only made comments about Moore and Dee, not even including Orsby in the mix; official COFO documents say nothing about such bodies; Rev. Ed King, Lawrence Guyot, Cleveland Sellers, Stokely Carmichael, Bob Zellner, James Farmer, James Forman, Unita Blackwell, Charles Cobb, and Rita Schwerner Bender, among others, either deny that other bodies were unearthed or are unaware of such claims.[217] One of the more interesting skeptics is not a "movement activist" per se, but a native Philadelphian, Florence Mars. In her important memoir on the Klan's supremacy in Neshoba County and her active resistance,

Witness in Philadelphia, she recounts the discovery of the Moore and Dee remains and makes no claims about additional bodies discovered during the search for the three missing men.[218]

As I've attempted to illustrate, the claim about unidentified Black bodies discovered during the search for Goodman, Schwerner, and Chaney has evolved in curious ways: the number of bodies has grown; the locations have been both specified and left vague; some were found during the search for the three while others were not; the Klan killed some, but unknown assailants killed others. Perhaps the most egregious and fantastic claim of all, though, comes from two newspaper articles in 2011 and 2012. The *Journal Gazette* of Fort Wayne, Indiana, published an account of Freedom Summer by married CORE activists George and Louise Smith, who had organized in their hometown of Meridian. "On the search for the three men," the author reports, "workers found five Black bodies in the river." While the "workers" in question are not identified and the "river" is not specified, Louise Smith is the first person, that I am aware of, to claim what happened next to the nameless five: "They just threw them back."[219] As if they were unwanted or out-of-season fish! In an article commemorating the forty-eighth anniversary of Freedom Summer the following year, Janus Adams of *The Advocate* (Stamford-Norwalk, Connecticut) adds an important detail to Smiths' claim: "Dredging up rivers and old wounds, FBI agents recovered other Black murder victims. These bodies, the agents threw back; buried unsung, unsought, under centuries of guilt."[220] The idea that the nation's leading law enforcement agency would "throw back" Black bodies as it searched for the white bodies of Goodman and Schwerner is horrifying—even as it serves as a telling barometer of race and memory in the age of Obama. Whether that memory functions rhetorically as a "look how far we've come" or something more sinister, the incredible claim is left unsourced—and also unchallenged.

That narrative, however unsourced and undocumented, perhaps shouldn't surprise us. The originating premise for Freedom Summer, after all, was that white lives would create more interest from the press—newspapers and television—the Justice Department, the FBI, and of course President Lyndon Johnson—especially if those young and white and educated bodies were harmed. It's hardly surprising, then, that part of the pushback against Freedom Summer—part of the resistance to the Goodman, Schwerner, and Chaney–dominated understanding of that foundational event—would take the form of asserting that Black lives matter, too. Had they mattered in roughly comparable ways, COFO wouldn't have needed a "white invasion" of Mississippi in the first place. And so as we look to the next fifty years of Freedom Summer historiography, many seek to re-represent the victims that summer—from a Holy and Interracial Trinity to those—how many?—written off that still predominantly white page.

But historical veracity might not really be the point: race and memory are. A historiography dominated by the search for two white men, within a much larger civil rights historiography in which Freedom Summer serves as a dramatic climax of the "short" civil rights movement, is ultimately a historiography dominated by white actors on the historical stage. SNCC and COFO understood as early as 1963 that bringing a huge influx of white students to Mississippi could change civil rights in the state; they likely did not know that a white-on-white murder would also change civil rights historiography. More than fifty years later, the "fact" that we still don't know even the names of the many Black bodies supposedly discovered functions rhetorically to request that we shift our focus away from the beguiling and now-familiar murders of Goodman, Schwerner, and Chaney in order to see anew how race has inflected our history and memory of "that summer."

That Freedom Summer has become something of a Holy American Moment in interracial democracy and color-blind justice perhaps shouldn't surprise us. In an age yearning for triumphal narratives of racial progress that might (finally) usher us into the post-racial era, COFO's Summer Project exists in very rare historiographic company. One of the more recent synoptic and popular histories of the Summer Project, by an author featured extensively in Stanley Nelson's PBS documentary, is Bruce Watson's 2010 book, *Freedom Summer*. Watson's take on that history is portended in the title following the colon: *The Savage Season That Made Mississippi Burn and Made America a Democracy*. Even as it riffs on the FBI's code name for its investigation—Miburn—and the Hollywood blockbuster that made headlines in 1988, the title is nothing if not causally optimistic. That is, because of COFO's interracial Summer Project, the United States finally fulfilled its civic destiny and became an (interracial) democracy. Such a title also riffs on SNCC communications director Julian Bond's satirical take on civil rights history: "Rosa sat down, Martin stood up, and the white kids came down and saved the day." Minus the white students' participation, so the logic goes, the country's civic destiny must await some future event.

But even putting aside for the moment the extravagances of Watson's title, his account further enshrines a view of the white volunteers originally put forward by sociologist Doug McAdam in his 1988 book, *Freedom Summer*.[221] That is, Watson and McAdam both locate the movements that would change the nation during the 1960s squarely in the annealing heat of a Mississippi summer. Whether it was the free-speech movement at Berkeley, the women's movement, the anti-war movement, or the coming sexual revolution, all the many seeds of progressive and New Left America were sown in the fertile Mississippi soil. "And in the forefront of each [movement] were veterans of Freedom Summer: who had seen democracy denied, who had watched 'the law' subjugate an entire people, and who had come home angry and disillusioned. For the rest of the 1960s, Mississippi would remain their benchmark of injustice, the place where one generation's American dream went to die," notes Watson. "Time and again, 1960s spokesmen . . . would refer to Mississippi as the school where they had learned to question America. And as protests became increasingly shrill, bewildered parents would ask why their children seemed so cynical about their country. The answer was easy. The children had been to Mississippi."[222] No doubt, many white Freedom Summer veterans helped lead the New Left on and off campus in the coming years. The great majority did not. But by emphasizing that so many progressive roads led back to the dusty trails and fetid swamps of 1964 Mississippi, Watson and McAdam stake their claim to a continuous historiography that locates white intercession as the sine qua non of progressive America.[223] That historiography often often leaves important Black activists and activism in the void. Perhaps not surprisingly, that historiography has also enshrined a heroic memory for various actors in the Summer Project drama—most notably the FBI and Goodman, Schwerner, and Chaney.

Back-Seat Driver

While big-budget films exploring America's long racial history are issued sporadically at best, popular films that attempt to portray moments during the civil rights movement (1954–65) are extraordinarily rare. That it took nearly fifty years to do a major film on Martin Luther King Jr. and the voting rights campaign in Selma—Ava DuVernay's *Selma*—is testament to such reluctance. The number of major Hollywood films can almost be counted on one hand: *The Long Walk Home* (1990), *Malcolm X* (1992), *Freedom Song* (2000), and *The Rosa Parks Story* (2002); perhaps we could include *Ghosts of Mississippi* (1996) and *The Butler* (2013) if we extend our temporal parameters. In sketching this admittedly cursory inventory, it's nonetheless remarkable that Freedom Summer has no fewer than three films—all of which focus intently on the murders of Goodman, Schwerner, and Chaney.[224]

Alan Parker's Oscar-winning 1988 film, *Mississippi Burning*, is perhaps the best-known civil rights movement–era film of all;[225] recently it was reissued in a special twenty-fifth anniversary DVD release, proof of the film's ongoing popularity and relevance.[226] Despite the film's box office draw and critical acclaim, the civil rights community collectively expressed its anger: the thinly fictionalized film glorified the FBI at the expense of the summer volunteers, Black organizers, and movement participants. Moreover, that glorification of an all-white and all-male organization that in reality had a most ambivalent, if not hostile, relationship to movement participants skewed historical understanding in favor of a federal government who, as we've seen, did almost nothing to protect summer volunteers prior to June 21. But the murders of the three men, captured in the film's opening, serve as the narrative fulcrum for what follows; minus the murders of two white men and their Black sidekick—and James Chaney is rendered as merely that in the film's opening—the film has no plot.[227] Viewers watch as the old-school and new-school FBI battle it out over forty-four days and two-plus hours in the efforts to crack the local Klan—which, of course, they eventually do with the help of seduction, money, and some timely torture. While some sort of justice is delivered by the movie's end—what, for whom, and for how long is never specified—*Mississippi Burning* closes with an arresting image: a defaced headstone in a sprawling cemetery reads, "1964 NOT FORGOTTEN." This overt memory marker pleads with the viewer not to forget the remarkable events of that summer—events that begin and end (thus the cemetery) with the murders of two white men. And a Black man riding in the back—literally. As the credits roll, the film reminds us that our act of viewing is simultaneously an act of memory. But our commitment to "not forget" is forged to a history of heroic white martyrdom and heroic white justice seekers—a history threatened by those who have already tried to deface and destroy it. Stated differently, our memories are tied to a very partial filmic rendering of Freedom Summer, one in which Black characters appear only as victims of history rather than agents of racial change, one in which James Chaney isn't even allowed to sit in the front seat, let alone drive.

Less than two years later, Hollywood found Freedom Summer again. Roger Young's *Murder in Mississippi* can be productively read as a rather direct rebuttal to *Mississippi Burning*, as the film focuses exclusively on the relationship between James Chaney and Mickey Schwerner. Instead of presenting him as a back-seat character, Blair Underwood's depiction of Chaney shows the CORE organizer and Meridian native to be passionate, intelligent, fearless, and ferocious; he is very much a mentor figure to an older, but often naive, Schwerner. In Young's version of the pivotal car-chase sequence, all three men are huddled together in the front seat—and James Chaney is driving, rather expertly. He is also the last to die as he attempts to protect and cradle his dying friends. Like *Mississippi Burning*, *Murder in Mississippi* closes with singing at a church, but unlike the heroic and white justice achieved in the former, closure is resisted in the latter. Before the credits roll we are informed that nobody served more than six years in jail, none of the Klansmen was ever tried on murder charges, and all are free today. Memory is troubled and unstable in that past racial injustices remain to be punished; the point is underscored in the last scene, in which James Chaney's brother, Ben, continues his activist mission. But even though *Murder in Mississippi* builds its story based on a complexly layered interracial friendship, the blunt fact remains: Goodman, Schwerner, and Chaney remain at the narrative center of Freedom Summer. If we are asked to remember anything from the summer of 1964, it's that two white men and a Black man were murdered and their killers remain free.

"Three of the volunteers . . ."

Hollywood isn't the only memory industry at work when it comes to Freedom Summer; both Ohio and Mississippi have created more material memory products to remember and commemorate the Summer Project. Perhaps not surprisingly, Goodman, Schwerner, and Chaney are quite literally imprinted and planted on the landscape (fig. 1). In April 2000, Miami University in Oxford, Ohio, formerly the Western College

Figure 1. Courtesy of Miami University Press and Dana Trilk.

for Women, officially dedicated its Freedom Summer Memorial. A tiered outdoor amphitheater situated between the university's chapel and the classrooms in which many training sessions were held, the memorial offers a chronological and spatial rendering of the Summer Project's key events.

Of the thirty-six separate limestone seats/panels, eleven directly or indirectly feature Goodman, Schwerner, and Chaney. The topmost seating panels announce the Summer Project to be held in Oxford, and subsequent ones slowly descend to the two climactic panels in the speaker's circle at the bottom of the amphitheater. They say, in part, that the memorial "honors the young volunteers involved in the historic voter registration drive of 1964 and symbolizes appreciation for the idealism of young people everywhere whose sacrifices have created a more just society." Without naming them, the memorial then celebrates the participants in Freedom Summer and the countless other "young people" who labor on behalf of a more just society. This very general attempt at commemoration calls to mind the Watson/McAdam historiographic claim about Freedom Summer's legacy: the Mississippi volunteers fundamentally reshaped the country as the 1960s unfolded.[228] The second closing panel is far more specific: "James Chaney, 21, Andrew Goodman, 20, and Michael Schwerner, 24, trained at Western College for Women before heading south to register Black voters as part

JAMES CHANEY, 21, ANDREW GOODMAN, 20, AND MICHAEL SCHWERNER, 24
TRAINED AT WESTERN COLLEGE FOR WOMEN BEFORE
HEADING SOUTH TO REGISTER BLACK VOTERS AS PART OF
THE MISSISSIPPI FREEDOM SUMMER PROJECT.
THEY LEFT OXFORD JUNE 20, 1964, AND
DISAPPEARED THE NEXT DAY IN MISSISSIPPI.
THEIR BODIES WERE FOUND BURIED IN AN
EARTHEN DAM SIX WEEKS LATER.

Figure 2. Courtesy of Miami University.

of the Mississippi Freedom Summer Project" (fig. 2). While the memorial celebrates their (future) work on behalf of Black voter registration—when in fact they were attempting to open a Freedom School at Mt. Zion Methodist Church—it also highlights their deaths. The panel closes, "They left Oxford June 20, 1964, and disappeared the next day in Mississippi. Their bodies were found buried in an earthen dam six weeks later." Fourteen years later, during the fiftieth anniversary celebration and conference, three trees adjacent to the memorial were planted and dedicated—one to each of the three murdered men.

All memorials, by dint of their commemorative function, are rhetorical, but the Oxford memorial is uniquely so: the design of the amphitheater is set to resemble a speaking rostrum facing a small and tiered audience that spreads out as we ascend its steps; in fact, the memorial committee uses the term "speaker's circle" to reference the final two panels. Too, the memorial is meant to be used and engaged; one has to sit on its many panels/seats in order to read the chronological narrative. One can rather easily envision the Freedom Summer Memorial as a meeting place on campus, one where speakers and listeners interact within an intimate shared circle amid a bucolic setting situated between the divine (Kumler Chapel) and the secular (Peabody Hall).

Presence, of course, always implicates absence—and the absences at Oxford are notable. First, nary a word is mentioned about the National Council of Churches and the last-minute rescheduling of the training sessions. Recall that the council encountered resistance from Berea College, thus the move to Oxford at a late hour; the gathering, in sum, was not without controversy. But that controversy is completely elided at the memorial. Absent, too, is any mention of COFO organizers, including Bob Moses, Dave Dennis, or other leaders in SNCC and CORE; beyond Goodman, Schwerner, and Chaney, only President Johnson is very briefly singled out by name in the three dozen panels. The memorial frequently makes mention of key violent episodes during the summer, but terms such as "young Negroes" or "Negro woman," a "group of Oxford residents," and "nine Negro homes" are used to refer to victims; violence, in other words, is systemic rather than episodic, but its victims are never named—save for the murdered men. The kidnap and murder of Henry Dee and Charles Moore is not mentioned or referenced, even as the memorial chronologically documents the accumulating violent reprisals. Also notable by omission is the fact that the Mississippi Freedom Democratic Party isn't referenced at all. In a memorial that conspicuously celebrates voter registration work, it's indeed troubling that the MFDP, arguably the apotheosis of Freedom Summer, is left in the commemorative void.

As if to underscore that this memorial is very much about three men and their violent deaths, the state of Ohio historical marker that fronts the memorial reads, in part, "Three of the volunteers—James Chaney of Mississippi, and Andrew Goodman and Michael Schwerner of New York—disappeared in rural Mississippi on June 21, 1964, mere days after leaving Oxford, Ohio. Their bodies were discovered forty-four days later, buried in an earthen dam. Ku Klux Klan members were later convicted on federal conspiracy charges" (fig. 3). While the three men dominate the historical marker, there is no mention that the men were in fact lynched by a police-Klan cabal. Too, the men did not "disappear" so much as they were kidnapped, shot, and then buried—all in a short period of time. White Mississippians in June and July of 1964 liked to claim that the three men had in fact "disappeared"—the better to claim that the entire thing was a hoax designed to attract media attention. Note that Freedom Summer also gets truncated to be a volunteer-led voting rights drive. As noted previously, the COFO Summer Project was far more than merely an attempt to

Figure 3. Courtesy of Miami University.

register African Americans to vote; by that one metric, the project would have been a miserable failure, since so few were able to successfully register.

That the narrative and commemorative focus is squarely on Goodman, Schwerner, and Chaney is hard to miss at Oxford—a point accentuated, as if it needed additional emphasis, by the three dogwood trees planted quite literally in their names during June 2014. Why the memorial needed additional commemorative landscaping and artwork fourteen years after its original unveiling remains a mystery. Not only does each of the three men have a tree in his memory, but at closer inspection a bronzed tree sculpture with inscription and wind chimes grows quite literally together with the dogwood tree (fig. 4). From the base of the sculpture and proceeding vertically, each begins with the age and name of the martyr it honors: "To 20 year old Andrew Goodman . . ." By calling attention to their ages at death, together with the seeming embrace of a living tree, the effect is to subtly merge life and death; the living dogwood grows with and around the sculpture to form a mosaic in which the two appear to the naked eye as one visible and dynamic memory marker. The deaths of the three men are rendered less as a static memory and more as an evolving present, one in which the future will look different than the past. The wind chimes function rhetorically as signifiers of euphonious speech; after all, they are

Figure 4. Courtesy of Miami University.

mere steps from the "speaker's circle," where Goodman, Schwerner, and Chaney's names are explicitly evoked. The three murdered men aren't quite alive in Oxford, Ohio, but the static engraved stone of the pavilion has been enlivened with a sonic treescape that quite demonstrably embraces the past—a past that looks, to most onlookers, quite alive.

In sum, then, the memorial work on campus in Oxford privileges the murders of three of the participants rather than the educational workshops and interracial training specific to those two historic weeks of June 1964. Such memory work is certainly in keeping with how Freedom Summer has been memorialized across many different contexts and places.

The state of Mississippi has erected three memorials on its landscape across nearly a quarter of a century related to the events of Freedom Summer—all three of which directly reference the murders of Goodman,

Figure 5. Courtesy of Corderion Stephens.

Schwerner, and Chaney. The first sign, dedicated during the twenty-fifth anniversary of the murders in 1989, and bearing the banner "Freedom Summer Murders," is located at Mt. Zion Methodist Church (fig. 5). Not only does Mt. Zion feature an anniversary service for the three men every June, but the Mississippi Department of Archives and History (MDAH) memorial also attempts to redeem their deaths: "On June 21, 1964, voting rights activists James Chaney, Andrew Goodman, and Michael Schwerner, who had come here to investigate the burning of Mt. Zion Church, were murdered. Victims of a Klan conspiracy, their deaths sparked national outrage and led to the first successful federal prosecution of a civil rights case in Mississippi."[229] The two events are not unrelated: the national outrage expressed in the aftermath of their deaths and the successful federal prosecution occupy the same sentence—and the same sentiments. Left unstated, but very much present: the skin color of Goodman and Schwerner engendered both reactions.

The commemorative marker at Mt. Zion proved insufficient for Mississippi's dynamic racial landscape: in consecutive years, two new signs were erected, one at the Neshoba County Jail, where the three men were held for nearly seven hours as the Klan cabal formed, and the second near the site

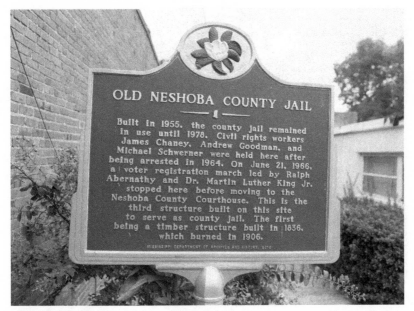

OLD NESHOBA COUNTY JAIL

Built in 1955, the county jail remained in use until 1978. Civil rights workers James Chaney, Andrew Goodman, and Michael Schwerner were held here after being arrested in 1964. On June 21, 1966, a voter registration march led by Ralph Abernathy and Dr. Martin Luther King Jr. stopped here before moving to the Neshoba County Courthouse. This is the third structure built on this site to serve as county jail. The first being a timber structure built in 1836, which burned in 1906.

Figure 6. Courtesy of RJ Fitzpatrick.

where they were murdered, on Rock Cut Road just south of Philadelphia. In 2012, an MDAH sign with the banner "Old Neshoba County Jail" was erected at the original site. The sign reads, in part, "Civil rights workers, James Chaney, Andrew Goodman, and Michael Schwerner were held here after being arrested in 1964" (fig. 6). Arguably the lack of narrative detail is precisely the point: visitors to this site are already familiar with the story. As a node in a much larger story, the sign doesn't need to repeat what many already know: why they were arrested, what was taking place while they were being held, and what happened upon their release. Moreover, we don't even need a specific date—June 21—or a context—Freedom Summer—since presumably those details are already well understood; "civil rights workers" is the only germane context here.

South of town, on State Highway 19, not insignificantly named the Chaney-Goodman-Schwerner Memorial Highway by an act of the Mississippi legislature in 2005, the MDAH installed a third Freedom Summer–themed sign in 2013; its banner reads "Goodman, Chaney and Schwerner Murder Site" (fig. 7). Even as it changes the alphabetical order of the three names, the sign also works hard to redeem their deaths—so hard, in fact, that it runs afoul of civil rights history. "On June 21, 1964, James Chaney,

Figure 7. Courtesy of RJ Fitzpatrick.

Andrew Goodman, and Michael Schwerner were murdered near here by members of the Ku Klux Klan and local law enforcement. They were volunteers for Mississippi Freedom Summer, a drive to register Black voters." While the Summer Project is accurately invoked as a context for the Klan's violent response, only Goodman was a volunteer, and we know that voter registration work was only part of the larger project. Small but important details. The sign then moves to a very troubling conclusion: "Though no one was indicted for their murder until 2005, the crime sparked national outrage that helped spur passage of the 1964 Civil Rights Act." Note again the phrase "national outrage," also used in Oxford, to motivate the federal response—in this case, passage of the Civil Rights Act. But the disappearance of Goodman, Schwerner, and Chaney, on June 21, in no way influenced passage of the landmark legislation: the House passed its version of the bill on February 10, 1964; the Senate passed its version on June 19; and the two bills were reconciled in committee on July 2, at which point Johnson quickly gave his signature. Regardless of the historical veracity of the most recent commemorative marker, the larger historiographic point remains: it took two white men to "disappear" (not yet die) in Mississippi before national civil rights legislation could be enacted; only "national outrage" caused by this event prompted the federal government to finally act.

Mississippi Goddam?

As noted, the state of Mississippi commissioned the three Freedom Summer markers, each of which was originally designed to be part of a larger
commemorative mosaic: the Mississippi Civil Rights Museum. That undertaking, nearly twenty years in the making, had its grand opening in December 2017. The museum, stunning in its design and incredibly ambitious in its
scope, has been very well received, with recognition from patrons around
the world. To no one's surprise, it has some things to say about the Summer
Project and its role in the larger movement for civil rights in Mississippi,
several of which bear on who gets remembered, how they get remembered,
and—always—who gets elided in that process. There is also a very curious
ambivalence on the question of unnamed Black bodies.

Patrons of the museum are asked to see the Freedom Vote as a necessary
first step for Freedom Summer, which would follow seven months later.
That is, before getting to a portico, dominated by Chaney, Goodman, and
Schwerner (the museum's ordering), patrons must pass by a detailed set of
panels featuring photographs and texts from the Freedom Vote; an office
is also recreated to simulate a busy COFO staging area. Not surprisingly,
the issue of white volunteers and Black activists is featured.

While the text of the panel accurately depicts the argument among
COFO's staff about whether or not to bring white college students into
Mississippi, note the photographs on the left. None of the three featured
picture panels shows any of the white student volunteers; Yale and Stanford
remain in the visual void, even as Allard Lowenstein's credentials are mis-
represented to include being a professor at Yale (fig. 8). A second Freedom
Vote panel reveals the effects of the campaign. Not surprisingly, interracial
tensions are featured even as memory makers ask patrons to look to 1964
and the Summer Project.

In a panel ostensibly dedicated to the achievements of the Freedom Vote,
there's a curious subject switch in mid-paragraph: from relatively poor
voting totals in Leflore County to how the media covered the campaign.
"Media coverage, when not dismissing the Freedom Vote as a sideshow,
focused on the white student volunteers. This fact annoyed those who
had opposed inviting the students, but Bob Moses saw it as a lesson. He
remarked that the election made it clear that 'the Negroes of Mississippi

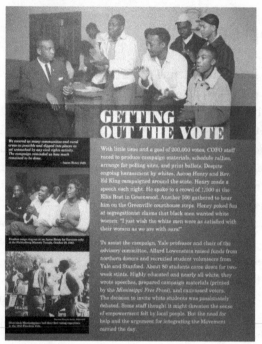

Figure 8. Courtesy of RJ Fitzpatrick.

will not get the vote until the equivalent of an army is sent here'" (fig. 9). As if to form a rebuttal to the whitewashed media coverage, this panel also features only Black men, women, and children. In fact, note the curious gap in the lower left: it appears as if a picture (featuring white volunteers?) has been removed altogether. Regardless of motive, the curators of the Freedom Vote exhibit are simply not going to feature visually the white volunteers from Yale or Stanford; the media's fixation with white students won't be duplicated here in 2017, nor presumably in perpetuity. Even the white lieutenant governor on the Freedom Ballot, Rev. Ed King, is notably absent from the images.

While items that foreshadow Freedom Summer are on display, before arriving at this space in the museum, patrons must pass by a small display featuring the photographs of four Black men: Louis Allen, whose murder on January 31, 1964, pushed Bob Moses to argue forcefully for the project; Mack Charles Parker, who was lynched in April of 1959 for the alleged rape of a white woman near Poplarville, Mississippi; and last, Thomas Moore of Colorado Springs, Colorado, holding a small picture of his younger brother,

Figure 9. Courtesy of RJ Fitzpatrick.

Figure 10. Courtesy of RJ Fitzpatrick.

Charles Moore (fig. 10). The photographs share no thematic linkages other than that three of the men were lynched by Mississippi white supremacists. Curious, too, is the photographic absence of Henry Hezekiah Dee, a photograph of whom does survive. Why Charles Moore's older brother is featured is not explained.

Three short paragraphs detail why each man died. Moore's account is most interesting on the question of missing Black bodies: "During the 1964 manhunt, the FBI discovered the bodies of Charles Moore, Henry Dee, and the body of a third unidentified man. Klansmen had abducted Moore and Dee and beaten them to death before tying their bodies to engine blocks and dumping them in the river." Readers are assumed to know what "manhunt" and "river" the text refers to, even as we've yet to arrive at the

Freedom Summer location in the museum. The factual errors repeat many 1964 news accounts: the FBI found the bodies while looking for Goodman, Schwerner, and Chaney, and Moore and Dee were both dead by the time their bodies were submerged in the Old River. Far more interesting is the historical claim that the FBI found a "third unidentified man." Would this be the unidentified body and/or torso in a CORE T-shirt? Or would this be an entirely new (presumably) Black man whom the FBI deliberately chose not to identify? And how could the Black body be unidentified if it's being identified in a museum space? Is this the Mississippi Civil Rights Museum's way of expressing its agnosticism on the veracity of finding Black bodies during the summer of 1964?

While the museum did not respond to my query requesting a source for the claim, I can't help but wonder if this is Cagin, Dray, and Dittmer recycled for museum consumption. Recall that these authors claimed that a "never identified" Black teenager had been hauled out of the Big Black River, also during the search for Goodman, Schwerner, and Chaney. All that seems to be missing from the museum's account is the CORE T-shirt and the age of the body. In a word, we know that body is fourteen-year-old Herbert Orsby of New Orleans, by way of Pickens, Mississippi, and the Big Black River.

The museum would seem to know that as well. In the main rotunda of the building, a space where people dance amid spectacular ribbons of light and a recording of "This Little Light of Mine," the mood is made somber by the fact that patrons are literally encircled by the names of martyrs who lost their lives in Mississippi because of racial violence. Emmett Till's name is there. Even the names of Henry Dee and Charles Moore circle the rotunda. And so, too, does the name "Herbert Orsby" (fig. 11).

When the museum opened, Orsby's first name was mistakenly printed as "Hubert." Not only was his first name initially wrong, but the date of his death remains in error. Has the "never identified" body, supposedly recovered by the FBI, finally been identified in the museum rotunda? Why does the Mississippi Civil Rights Museum need more lynched Black bodies? When the FBI closed its case on April 12, 2010, they concluded that Herbert Orsby very likely drowned, on September 7, when he was last seen leaving his grandparents' house close to the Big Black River.[230] The state of Mississippi would have us believe otherwise, making him a victim of racial violence.

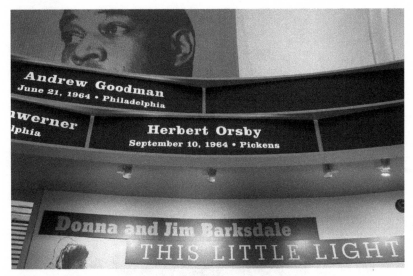

Figure 11. Courtesy of RJ Fitzpatrick.

The next space in the museum brings visitors at long last to the Summer Project. Sort of. In two very distinct presentations, Goodman, Schwerner, and Chaney's story is told. The first tableau features three vertically stacked and somewhat crudely drawn (police?) sketches of the men with identifying names (fig. 12). An accompanying contextualizing flier in the upper right of the presentation offers smaller, horizontal photographic images of the three men with the heading "MISSING CALL FBI." Both the sketches and flier are further framed by a beaten-up green lunch pail with two stickers attached to it, and a typewriter with a sheet of paper suggesting an in-progress document. The scene might well be an early FBI work space or a makeshift area occupied by a member of the press (fig. 13). There's a third possibility: this might also be a COFO office in Jackson, as several additional fliers are in fact actual press releases put out by the organization after the men went missing on June 21. All of this suggests that the preferred subject position for the visitor is that of searcher: we are being hailed to help look for the missing men, or at minimum to be on the lookout for them. Nothing in this interesting tableau suggests that the men are in fact dead, buried underneath a massive earthen dam on the Old Jolly Farm south and west of downtown Philadelphia. The stickers affixed to the lunch pail, "Witness in Philadelphia," help us narrow our search geographically, but we're searching all the same.

Figure 12. Courtesy of RJ Fitzpatrick.

Figure 13. Courtesy of RJ Fitzpatrick.

Figure 14. Courtesy of RJ Fitzpatrick.

As we move to our right, that mission seems to get more urgent with a dark and jagged constellation of images surrounded and centered by the text "Chaney, Goodman & Schwerner: Missing." Instead of images of fire—this is the "Miburn" case, after all—the museum features photographic images and text superimposed onto shards of fractured glass (fig. 14). Viewers once again see the three-panel horizontal shot of the missing men, and they are quite literally surrounded by black-and-white images: moving clockwise from the lower left, aerial photos of FBI men excavating bodies, members of the US Navy dragging a muddy river, more aerial photos of the Jolly Farm excavation, the burned-out station wagon discovered in the Bogue Chitto Swamp, the charred remains of the Mt. Zion Church, a close-up of Dave Dennis speaking at James Chaney's funeral in Meridian on August 7, and Chaney's mom, Fannie Lee Chaney, consoling her youngest son, Ben, at said funeral.

So, who exactly is missing at this point, and what should visitors be searching for? The visual evidence strongly suggests that the bodies have been quite literally unearthed. Interestingly, the death of James Chaney dominates this prominent presentation at the MCRM. Where, for example, are the parents and family members of Mickey Schwerner and Andrew

Goodman? Where are the speakers who eulogized their lives, and where are the excerpts from their speeches?

The most prominently displayed person in this exhibit, ironically, is not one of the three murdered civil rights workers; rather, it's CORE's Dave Dennis, who helped organize Neshoba County, worked very closely with Mickey and Rita Schwerner, and save for a bad bout of bronchitis might well have been with the three men that fateful Sunday. The blue Ford Fairlane station wagon that the men used was registered in his name. A profile shot of Dennis, full throated and with neck muscles tensed, is featured in the upper right-hand corner. Unless visitors know their civil rights history rather well, they simply aren't going to know who this young man speaking in a jean jacket is. The far upper left of the presentation's dimly lit text reads, "I'm sick and tired of going to the funerals of Black men who have been murdered by white men. I've got vengeance in my heart, and I ask you to feel angry with me." The quote is attributed to Dave Dennis. Again, visitors will need to do some major interpretive work to connect the image of Dennis with the eulogy he delivered at James Chaney's funeral; there is simply nothing intuitive about the panels to suggest that this is Dave Dennis, and that he's speaking at James Chaney's funeral.

But did Dave Dennis in fact utter these words at the funeral? The racially loaded statement suggests that the speaker and his interlocutors/visitors are justified in seeking to avenge the death of James Chaney. In a movement whose nonviolent ethos was a constant refrain and a powerful means of persuasion, Dave Dennis seems to have crossed the threshold into targeted retribution of white racists. Fortunately, we can check the highlighted and inflammatory quote for the simple reason that the press was at the service, and in the words of Dave Dennis during an interview for *Eyes on the Prize*, he saw sobbing Ben Chaney in a front pew and "lost it." Dennis's speech has been frequently anthologized and appears in several civil rights documentaries—for his incredible passion, for his sense of deep fatigue and anger, for his tearful near-collapse in mid-sentence at the abrupt close, and for quite literally saying to his audience near the end of his speech that if they go home and just "take" another murder without doing something about it, then "God damn your souls." In brief, Dennis's eulogy has become part of the larger rhetorical history of the movement, and certainly a Freedom Summer touchstone.

From a recording of the address, it is clear the relevant part of the speech is quite different than the quote featured at the MCRM. Dennis stated, "I'm sick and tired of going to memorials. I'm sick and tired of going to funerals. I've got a bitter vengeance in my heart tonight. And I'm sick and tired and can't help but feel and I'm not going to stand here and ask anybody here not to be angry tonight."[231] In a word, the Mississippi Civil Rights Museum has taken some rather egregious liberties with Dave Dennis's eulogy. The recording and transcript are easily accessible, so why not get the quote right? Why make racially explicit that which was only implicit? Why take Dennis's very personal emotions and coax them onto his audience? The larger question, moreover, remains: What rhetorical function is achieved by the museum's blatant misrepresentation of Dave Dennis's speech? To skew the speech so badly in a particular direction—of Black-on-white extrajudicial violence and perhaps even murder—suggests some troubling possibilities, one of which involves Freedom Summer historiography. That is, by largely downplaying the deaths—far more the fact of their missing—of white volunteer Andrew Goodman and white CORE organizer Mickey Schwerner, the museum editorializes rather loudly that a Black James Chaney's death authorizes the possibility of a racially inflected, collective, and violent response. By privileging Chaney's death and funeral at this very prominent and new site to the history and memory of Freedom Summer, the MCRM can be seen speaking back to a historiographical tradition steeped almost exclusively in the primacy and importance of white bodies.

As I've documented, Dave Dennis was also one of the very first veterans of the Summer Project to make public the missing Black bodies claim, first in 1977 and steadily in the years since. The MCRM takes a very measured approach to that question in 2018. Under the three black-and-white photographs of Goodman, Schwerner, and Chaney at the "Missing" exhibit, signage explains that "the bodies of two Black Mississippians, Charles Moore and Henry Dee, were found during the massive manhunt as the FBI and news media swarmed." Not only is the statement accurate, but the MCRM is one of the very few commenting on Moore and Dee to correctly note that the FBI didn't find their bodies while searching for the three missing men. That said, a discerning reader is left to still wonder about the "third, unidentified man" specified in the preceding panel exhibit. In sum, the silence of the museum space on the possibility of many missing Black bodies suggests that the state of Mississippi rejects that claim.

And yet the official K–12 public school curriculum on the museum's website offers a different conclusion. Published in 2014 and copyrighted by the Mississippi Department of Archives and History, Lesson Five features fourteen pages on Freedom Summer, including this short paragraph: "On June 24 [sic], the Freedom Summer Project made national news due to the disappearance of three young civil rights workers, James Chaney, an African American Mississippian, and Michael Schwerner, and Andrew Goodman (northerners of Jewish decent [sic]). The FBI found their bodies buried beneath an earthen dam approximately six weeks later. During the course of the investigation, the bodies of eight other African American men were found, three of whom were known civil rights activists; the remaining five have never been identified."[232] The school curriculum sponsored, and thus approved, by the MCRM not only registers a verdict on the Black bodies claim, but it goes one step further to specify that three of these Black male bodies belonged to civil rights workers. If that is indeed the case, presumably we would know exactly who they are by dint of their identification as civil rights workers; in brief, they would each have names. And yet no names are revealed, no sources cited, nor are any dates and places detailed. High school students in Mississippi, and perhaps well beyond, are thus learning the history of Freedom Summer from a lesson plan that presently cannot be squared with the history presented inside the museum.

"James, Andrew, and Michael . . ."

Two final, and very important, commemorative events are important to note. Former president Barack Obama, our nation's first Black president and a dedicated student of civil rights history, has officially celebrated the legacy of Goodman, Schwerner, and Chaney on two different occasions and in two very different ways. In September 2010, and with unanimous votes in both the House and the Senate, a new FBI building in Jackson, Mississippi, was dedicated as the James Chaney, Andrew Goodman, Michael Schwerner, and Roy K. Moore Building. Moore had organized the opening of FBI's Jackson office in July 1964 and helped lead the investigation about the missing men. Doubtless the irony was not lost on movement veterans in particular: the very agency that vowed not to protect them ahead of the Summer Project ends up bearing their names forty-six years later. That the votes were unanimous in our very fractious political times, and bearing no small racial weight, is a profound testament to an irresistible public memory.

That memory was further codified by presidential proclamation on November 24, 2014, when all three men were awarded the nation's highest civilian honor: the Presidential Medal of Freedom. As part of the ongoing fiftieth anniversary of Freedom Summer, President Obama burnished further the names of the heroic three men into our collective national memory: "On June 21, 1964, three young men—two white, one Black—set out to learn more about the burning of a church in Neshoba County, Mississippi: James Earl Chaney, 21 years old; Andrew Goodman, 20 years old; and Michael Henry Schwerner, 24 years old. Young men. And in that Freedom Summer, these three Americans refused to sit on the sidelines. Their brutal murder by a gang of Ku Klux Klan members shook the conscience of our nation. It took 44 days to find their bodies, 41 years to bring the lead perpetrator to justice." The "national outrage" of Ohio and Mississippi memorials is here rendered by the president as something that "shook the conscience of our nation." No doubt many movement veterans applauded the president for his remarks—and couldn't help but miss the fact of the men's race, a point carefully highlighted by Obama.

He continued, "And while they are often remembered for how they died, we honor them today for how they lived—with the idealism and the courage of youth. James, Andrew, and Michael could not have known the impact they would have on the Civil Rights Movement or on future generations. And here today, inspired by their sacrifice, we continue to fight for the ideals of equality and justice for which they gave their lives. Today we are honored to be joined by James's daughter Angela, Andrew's brother David, and Michael's wife, Rita."[233] The president's rhetorical intimacy—"James, Andrew, and Michael"—serves, again, as a telling measure of the men's familiarity to our ongoing and collective national civil rights memory. While we know them with a familiar six-syllable cadence, we also know them by their first names.

Memory work, whether of a high and official cast such as the Presidential Medal of Freedom, or of a low and unofficial popular culture bent such as songs and big-budget films, is always imbricated with history;

memory's public face simply can't exist without a corresponding history. Not surprisingly, so much of the historiography surrounding Freedom Summer is dominated by the deaths of the three men. As Ed King, who served on the front lines in 1964, recently noted, the murders "have become perhaps the one story most associated with Freedom Summer."[234] Moreover, in a historiographical tradition that typically divides the short civil rights movement into roughly ten parts—the *Brown* Supreme Court decision, the Emmett Till murder, the Montgomery bus boycott, school integration in Little Rock, student sit-ins, the Freedom Rides, Meredith's integration of Ole Miss, the Birmingham campaign, Freedom Summer, and the Selma voting rights campaign—COFO's summer of 1964 dominates the time line.[235] While each has been given significant attention by historians— academic and popular—Freedom Summer's extended literature dwarfs the others. Dittmer's "That Summer" is most apt here; more than twenty-five years after his chapter in *Local People*, that sentiment is stronger than ever. Whether in the form of memoirs from activists and volunteers, articles, book chapters, monographs, sourcebooks, textbooks, collected letters, collected journalism, or legal documents, the literature about Freedom Summer is vast—and continues to grow. Within that sizable body, the story of Goodman, Schwerner, and Chaney proliferates and dominates; it is "depressingly familiar" by dint of its near-constant repetition as the summer of 1964 unfolds. Just as the story riveted the nation and the world then, the story's appeal in the present is unabated.

In what is perhaps the most familiar story in a civil rights movement historiographical tradition dominated by Freedom Summer, we can also glimpse the vexations of race. As I've documented, the story of Goodman, Schwerner, and Chaney and the "national outrage" that attended it was largely, if not exclusively, a function of race. Bob Moses knew this in November 1963 even as Black COFO workers reluctantly agreed with it by June 1964. They have lived with that "national outrage," the "shaking of our conscience," per Obama, ever since.

Concomitant with the memorialization and historiographical dominance of the deaths of Goodman, Schwerner, and Chaney, we have glimpsed a second tradition, one far more muted but tenaciously demonstrable all the same; it attempts to talk back to that dominant tradition by invoking five unnamed Black bodies, eight unnamed Black bodies, more than a dozen unnamed Black bodies, Black bodies in trees, Black bodies by the sides of roads, headless Black bodies wearing CORE T-shirts, Black bodies in swamps. It beseeches us to write their history, to train our focus less on the Martyred Three and retrain it on the nameless others whose history (and names) remains in the void—the "wrong" bodies of Mississippi's "savage season" and beyond. The veracity of the claim, the historicity of the specifics, is far from the point; proof, after all, resides in the grainy black-and-white footage from July 12 and 13 at the Old River. Weren't these mutilated skeletal remains all the proof that was needed? Why do Goodman, Schwerner, and Chaney *still* need to dominate the story? The names Charles Moore, Henry Dee, and even Herbert Orsby distract us from the truth of the matter: white lives were the only ones that really mattered in 1964. More than fifty years later, the three civil rights workers' lives still matter more in our collective memory and our historiography.

Near the close of his remarkable life, writing about the Atlanta child murders, James Baldwin recalled a moment from 1964: "Some years ago, after the disappearance of civil rights workers Chaney, Goodman, and Schwirner [*sic*] in Mississippi, some friends of mine were dragging the river for their bodies. This one wasn't Schwirner [*sic*]. This one wasn't Goodman. This one wasn't Chaney. Then, as Dave Dennis tells it, 'It suddenly struck us—what difference did it make that it wasn't *them? What are these bodies doing in the river?*'"[236] Baldwin's memories are telling: "some years ago" and "some friends" tip us off that the historical specifics aren't terribly important to the story. Nor is the number of bodies or the specific river being dragged. Rather, the rhetorical function of Baldwin's brief anecdote is precisely to question a racial calculus in which Black bodies always come up wrong and anonymous in the search for the Martyred Three, then and now—a questioning that reveals its frustration and anger, perhaps, in a rather revealing misspelling.

Surely some might object and counter that the specific claims about nameless Black bodies made by movement veterans such as Dave Dennis, Hollis Watkins, Mary King, Charles McDew, Heather Tobis Booth, Allen Cooper, Jim Dann, John Lewis, and Ben Chaney, among others, is beside the point; their larger critique is that murdered Black men in Mississippi matter/mattered far less—to the nation, to the press, to the federal government—than murdered white men. Only a (white?) pedant would insist on such specificity when you're talking about Mississippi's long history of genocidal racism, after all. Too, shouldn't we, at minimum, sympathize with movement veterans' memories? Surely studies of traumatic memories indicate that such awful events as mass murder often get misremembered in the form of exaggeration.[237] Aren't you making just a bit too much out of this?

Fragile and Furtive Memory in Meadville

I'm standing on the south side of Main Street, on the west side of Meadville, Mississippi. The articles said I should look for Della Mae's Diner before Main Street snakes back to Highway 84. Sure enough, the shuttered diner is exactly where it's supposed to be. I exit my car to get a few pictures; on the other side of the street is the precise spot where Henry Dee and Charles Moore were hitchhiking when they were kidnapped by James Ford Seale and later murdered by the Bunkley Klansmen; this was their last place of freedom, where they joked with friends and looked forward to a sunny spring Saturday. As I steady my smartphone to get a few pictures, I notice a curious thing: there appears to be some sort of small structure directly across the road from where I'm standing. I strain my eyes to take a closer look. Sure enough, there appears to be a small black stand supporting two pictures. My pulse quickens. I hadn't heard or read anything about a memorial—makeshift or otherwise—for Henry Dee and Charles Moore. Crossing the highway, I see that it is in fact something of a vernacular, private memorial (fig. 15). A circular black tablet with white text is captioned "In Memory of," and under it reads, "Henry Hezekiah Dee & Charles Eddie Moore." In three short sentences their story is told: "Kidnapped by the Ku Klux Klan near this spot on May 2, 1964. Dee and Moore were later beaten, attached to iron weights and drowned in the Old Mississippi River. Their partial remains were first discovered on July 12 & 13, 1964." Under the text are two oval-shaped black-and-white pictures affixed to a square black placard, and I recognize that the picture on the left is Moore, the picture on the right is Dee. Resting on the ground, sandwiched between plastic flowers and emergent spring weeds, is a third black placard, which memorializes the two men who placed it in this unpretentious spot: "Original plaque built and erected on this spot by Thomas Moore [Charles's older brother] & David Ridgen" [a Canadian filmmaker]. The brief narrative continues, "Through their efforts Klansman James Ford Seale was indicted, tried and

In Memory of
Henry Hezekiah Dee
&
Charles Eddie Moore

Kidnaped by the Ku Klux Klan near this spot on May 2, 1964.
Dee and Moore were later beaten,
attached to iron weights, and drowned
in the old Mississippi River.
Their partial remains
were first discovered
on July 12, & 13, 1964.

Figure 15. Courtesy of RJ Fitzpatrick.

convicted. May Thomas' and David's quest for justice together be repeated
again and again by those that follow." As I photograph the largely camou-
flaged memorial, I become aware of east- and westbound traffic coming in
and out of Meadville. I also become aware of another fact as I reenter my
car: I would have never noticed the memorial had I not pulled over and
looked north across the street from Della Mae's; it is simply not observable
from the east or west.

I wondered, Why would this homemade memorial point south? Why
didn't it advertise itself just a bit more prominently? The answer arrived in
an email from David Ridgen a few weeks later: the sign had already been

stolen and/or destroyed three times. Somehow this seemed sadly fitting: Even in death, someone was trying to render Charles Moore and Henry Dee invisible and deny them a privately public commemoration on the landscape—just two nameless Black bodies murdered in 1964 somewhere in Mississippi. To give the two young men a name and a place, a very humble history and a memory, was simply too much for some. Fifty years and beyond.

Ridgen and Moore's story, and their quest for justice, is documented in the haunting 2007 film *Mississippi Cold Case*.[238] The film was released just before the Seale case went to trial; Ridgen first learned about the murders of Moore and Dee by watching a 1964 Canadian Broadcast Corporation (CBC) documentary, *Summer in Mississippi*. The CBC, along with many others, had rushed to the Old River following word of the Bowleses' discovery on July 12 and recorded the macabre removal of two corpses. Ridgen was curious to know: Just whose bodies were the so-called wrong bodies in the search for Goodman, Schwerner, and Chaney? Whose bodies did those bones belong to, anyway? What secrets did those bones and body bags hold? And so, having tracked down Charles Moore's brother in Colorado Springs and having convinced him to travel back to Mississippi and pursue justice for the two young murdered friends, Ridgen skillfully tells their story of improbable justice, from the dark woods of the Homochitto National Forest to the country homes of Charles Marcus Edwards and James Ford Seale, the murky waters of the Old River and Parker's Landing, and the humble brick church, Bunkley Baptist. And always traveling with them is the transcript of the FBI's 1964 investigation. COFO, Freedom Summer, and Goodman, Schwerner, and Chaney serve only as a necessary beginning, not as a narrative focus and frame. Safely bracketed from civil rights historiography and the looming shadow of the white Summer Project volunteers, Ridgen and Moore can finally tell the young men's stories. The right bodies can perhaps finally rest.

Instead of heading on to our destination in Natchez, I hang a right on McNair Road, just yards from the makeshift memorial in Meadville. And then a quick left onto Kirby Road. Since we are here, why not pay our respects at the cemetery behind Mt. Olive Church in the tiny hamlet of Kirby. Both men, I'd read, were buried nearby. Despite our best efforts we could not locate either man's grave. I was later informed that the location of both headstones is a tightly guarded secret, known only by family. Even in death, the bodies of Henry Dee and Charles Moore are shrouded in mystery and potential danger, submerged somewhere in the clay soil of Franklin County. Perhaps one day we will mark their graves and memorialize their lives in the most visible of ways, freed from the shadows of Mississippi and a collective memory and history that renders them as merely a proof, a sign of insignificance as we look for the three missing civil rights workers.

Perhaps that day will be upon us sooner than we think. At the National Civil Rights Memorial in Montgomery, Alabama, Maya Lin's circle of martyrs features forty men, women, and children murdered between 1955 and 1968 whose deaths were either a function of civil rights activity or meant to halt it. Nestled in black granite at the nation's self-appointed shrine to its civil rights martyrs, and situated between the names Bruce Klunder and Chaney, Goodman, and Schwerner, are Henry Hezekiah Dee and Charles Eddie Moore. Even as the national memorial, too, gets wrong that "their bodies were found during a massive search for the missing civil right workers, Chaney, Goodman, and Schwerner," the two Black teenagers from Franklin County, forever nineteen, have achieved their full names in death. Finally.

Coda: Naming Black Bodies in 2020 and Beyond

I originally drafted this monograph in 2016, not long after the fifty-year anniversary of Freedom Summer rhetorically spawned another round of unidentified Black bodies—without evidence or citation. In the ensuing years when this project was largely fallow, I noted that the claims continued to proliferate; anonymous Black bodies had almost become a trope for what happened during the Summer Project. Whether on a Wikipedia page for Freedom Summer, a book by movement volunteer-turned-filmmaker Jon Else, or yet another memoir of "that summer" authored by Lee Anna Sherman, the unidentified Black bodies from 1964 remain so in perpetuity, it seems.[239] And, we should add, uninvestigated.

The most recent permutation of the claim, though, perhaps portends a different possibility, one in which Black bodies are not only named, investigated, and celebrated, but perhaps even prosecuted. We would do well to celebrate the irony of this permutation: it is advanced by none other than

Dave Dennis Jr., the son of the CORE activist who gave so much initial energy and credibility to the unidentified Black bodies claim.

Following the publicity attending the three tectonic deaths in 2020 of Ahmaud Arbery, Breonna Taylor, and George Floyd, Dennis authored a lengthy essay for *The Atlantic*; its first paragraph begins, "**Black people disappear in America.** This fact is woven into the fabric of our country. Parents are separated from their children at slave auctions, never to be seen by them again. A loved one is here one day and turns up in the Jim Crow woods the next, dangling from trees under the cover of nightfall and inhumanity." Dennis Jr. then turns autobiographical: "I grew up with my father telling me stories of the 1964 Freedom Summer in which three activists—Andrew Goodman, Mickey Schwerner, and James Chaney, the sole African American in the group—went missing for 44 days after driving down a dark road in Neshoba County, Mississippi." Students of Freedom Summer and David Dennis Sr.'s role in it can sense what's coming. "The part of the story that most haunts my father, though, is that during all those weeks of looking for the three men, search parties discovered so many forgotten Black bodies in Mississippi ditches and swamps. 'Nobody was even looking for them anymore,' my dad would say. The echoes of those silenced Black voices reverberate through my family's bones." The title of the essay—"Ahmaud Arbery Will Not Be Erased"—foreshadows the essay's thrust: the young Black man who liked to jog through Brunswick, Georgia, neighborhoods, and who was allegedly lynched for it by three white men, will not be forgotten. No, Dave Dennis Jr.'s genealogical inheritance makes this rhetorical mission urgent: he must speak back to the void, to a history of Black erasure, silence, and thus forgetting. Despite his claim that "Black bodies in America remain disposable," they won't remain anonymous—if he has anything to say about it.[240]

David Dennis Jr. is but one author, with one keyboard. But perhaps the public lynching, in particular, of George Floyd, whose excruciatingly cruel death was captured on a cell phone and shared around the world, might move us well beyond the possibility of police reforms, and into journalistic and historical reforms, too. Perhaps one day soon we will tell the story of Hubert/Herbert Oarsby/Orsby and not only get his name and what he was wearing when he left his grandparents' house right, but also tell the story of his life, his family, his classmates—anything to suggest that his life wasn't disposable, or mattered only as another bullet point on a press release, incident report, or a museum Wall of Martyrs. Maybe when we try to teach and (re)write the story of Freedom Summer, we will expand it to include the Freedom Fall and Winter that preceded and succeeded it, one in which Goodman-Schwerner-Chaney aren't an apotheosis or a narrative fulcrum, but a chapter in a larger whole.

Yes, white lives mattered fundamentally to Bob Moses's mission of bringing the country to Mississippi in 1964. That mission was successful in ways that likely horrified him, that no doubt "rested heavy." What ought to "rest heavy" with the sons and daughters, the grandsons and grand-daughters of Freedom Summer, is the too-easy cliché, the facile "facts" that everybody already knows, the too-obvious conclusion that white Mississippians enforced their murderous white supremacy on generations of Black bodies. Yes, we hear the tortured incredulity of Dennis's father—"What are these bodies doing in the river"!?—and the story that each body might tell. By refusing to tell those stories, by simply repeating the number—five, eight, a dozen, or bodies too numerous to count—we tacitly acknowledge that yes, nameless Black bodies—then and now—are disposable. May that rest heavy, too.

NOTES

1. For a history of Brierfield Plantation, see Frank Edgar Everett Jr., *Brierfield: Plantation Home of Jefferson Davis* (Jackson: University Press of Mississippi, 1971).

2. Details about the discovery of Charles Moore's and Henry Dee's bodies are culled from several sources, including Harry N. MacLean, *The Past Is Never Dead: The Trial of James Ford Seale and Mississippi's Struggle for Redemption* (New York: Basic Books, 2009); and Alex A. Alston Jr. and James L. Dickerson, *Devil's Sanctuary: An Eyewitness History of Mississippi Hate Crimes* (Chicago: Lawrence Hill, 2009), 129–43. Some of the best local reporting on the case was done by the *Vicksburg Evening-Post*; see Pete Finlayson and Bob Wilder, "Second Body of Man Found in Tallulah Area," *Vicksburg Evening-Post*, July 13, 1964, 1, 12; Pete Finlayson, "Navy Divers Are Probing Muddy Offshoot of River," *Vicksburg Evening-Post*, July 14, 1964, 1; Finlayson, "Probe Continued by Navy Divers," *Vicksburg Evening-Post*, July 15, 1964, 1; Finlayson, "Waters Hide Secret in Mystery Deaths," *Vicksburg Evening-Post*, July 16, 1964, 1.

3. The United Press International (UPI), in particular, claimed initially that the body discovered by the Bowleses on Sunday was white and that it might be the corpse of Mickey Schwerner; see "Find Body with Feet Bound 17 Mi. S Tallulah," *Natchez Democrat*, July 13, 1964, 1.

4. In their fascinating phone conversation, Johnson initially stated that he had heard that one of the three missing civil rights workers' bodies had been recovered. Hoover corrected Johnson that no, in fact neither of the two bodies belonged to Goodman, Schwerner, or Chaney. But importantly, Hoover also notes that a civil rights investigation into the deaths of Moore and Dee was pending. As it turned out, that investigation was absolutely crucial to the arrest, trial, and conviction of Klansman James Ford Seale, more than forty years later. See http://web2.millercenter.org/lbj/audiovisual/whrecordings/telephone/con versations/1964/lbj_wh6407_07_4221.wav.

5. Several newspapers were keen to report that neither Moore nor Dee was involved in civil rights work, and thus not part of the "summer invasion." See "Navy Divers Scan River for Portions of Bodies," *Meridian Star*, July 15, 1964, 1, 2; and Leon Daniel (UPI), "'Good Negroes' Die Violently," *Jackson Daily News*, July 15, 1964, 21.

6. SNCC'ers is the preferred moniker of SNCC veterans.

7. Fleming notes that "the murders of Chaney, Goodman, and Schwerner have achieved nearly iconic status in recollections of the movement"; see Julius B. Fleming Jr., "'Living Proof of Something So Terrible': Pearl Cleage's *Bourbon at the Border* and the Politics of Civil Rights History and Memory," *Southern Quarterly* 52, no. 1 (2014): 202.

8. For an excellent rhetorical analysis of the visual power of the 1963 Birmingham campaign, see Davi Johnson, "Martin Luther King Jr.'s Birmingham Campaign as Image Event," *Rhetoric & Public Affairs* 10, no. 1 (2007): 1–25.

9. John Dittmer, *Local People: The Struggle for Civil Rights in Mississippi* (Urbana: University of Illinois Press, 1994), 115.

10. Dittmer, *Local People*, 109.

11. For various iterations of this story, narrated in her Hamer's words, see Maegan Parker Brooks and Davis W. Houck, eds., *The Speeches of Fannie Lou Hamer: To Tell It Like It Is* (Jackson: University Press of Mississippi, 2011). For the best biographical treatment of Hamer, see Kay Mills, *This Little Light of Mine: The Life of Fannie Lou Hamer* (Lexington: University of Kentucky Press, 2007). For Hamer as a rhetorician, see Maegan Parker Brooks, *A Voice That Could Stir an Army: Fannie Lou Hamer and the Rhetoric of the Black Freedom Movement* (Jackson: University Press of Mississippi, 2014).

12. For an excellent historical treatment of the Citizens' Council movement, see Neil R. McMillen, *The Citizens' Council: Organized Resistance to the Second Reconstruction, 1954–1964* (Urbana: University of Illinois Press, 1971).

13. In testimony before the US Senate on February 28, 1957, Belzoni, Mississippi, grocer Gus Courts recounted the threats made on his life by local members of the Citizens' Council in Humphreys County. If he did not cease his voter registration work, the council warned Courts, he would end up like his close friend, Rev. George W. Lee, who'd been murdered while driving home on May 7, 1955, in Belzoni. "They told me 'we're not going to let Negroes vote and we're not going to let the N.A.A.C.P. operate.' They told me, 'You're leading the Negroes in trying to get them to register and we're going to put you out of business.'" "Negro Testifies on Voting Abuse," *New York Times*, March 1, 1957, 9; see also Gus Courts, letter to sheriff of Humphrey[s] County, January 24, 1956, Papers of the National Association for the Advancement of Colored People, Part 20, White Resistance and Reprisals, 1956–1965, reel 1. Sheriff Ike Shelton, who investigated the case, infamously claimed that the buckshot lodged in Lee's jaw was simply loose dental fillings caused by the car crash. The FBI investigated Lee's murder and tentatively identified two council members, Peck Ray and Joe David Watson Sr., as suspects. The case, though, was never brought before a grand jury.

14. Quoted in Wesley C. Hogan, *Many Minds, One Heart: SNCC's Dream for a New America* (Chapel Hill: University of North Carolina Press, 2007), 144.

15. Quoted in William Chafe, *Never Stop Running: Allard Lowenstein and the Struggle to Save American Liberalism* (Princeton, NJ: Princeton University Press, 1998), 181.

16. Robert Moses, interview in *American Experience: 1964*, directed by Stephen Ives, (Washington, DC: Corporation for Public Broadcasting, 2014).

17. Charles M. Payne, *I've Got the Light of Freedom: The Organizing Tradition and the Mississippi Freedom Struggle* (Berkeley: University of California Press, 1995), 392.

18. Payne, *I've Got the Light of Freedom*, 394.

19. Chafe, *Never Stop Running*, 181.

20. For the origins of constitutive rhetoric in the field of speech and communication, see Richard B. Gregg, "The Ego-Function of the Rhetoric of Protest," *Philosophy and Rhetoric* 4, no. 2 (1971): 71–91. For a later and more oft-cited work, see Maurice Charland, "Constitutive Rhetoric: The Case of the *peuple québécois*," *Quarterly Journal of Speech* 73, no. 2 (1987): 133–50.

21. Robert Moses, interview by Joseph Sinsheimer, November 19, 1983, https://library .duke.edu/digitalcollections/media/jpg/sinsheimerjoseph/pdf/sinsio2005.pdf.

22. For a detailed history of the 1890 Mississippi State Constitutional Convention, see Dorothy Overstreet Pratt, *Sowing the Wind: The Mississippi Constitutional Convention of 1890* (Jackson: University Press of Mississippi, 2017).

23. Registering Black voters proved so difficult that the Voter Education Project, led by Wiley Branton and the Southern Regional Council, which had financed a great deal of COFO's work in Mississippi, pulled its funding in the fall of 1963. The paltry number of successful Black registrants simply did not warrant the expenditure.

24. Robert Moses, interview by Joseph Sinsheimer, November 19, 1983.

25. For the only comprehensive histories on the Freedom Vote, see Joseph A. Sinsheimer, "The Freedom Vote of 1963: New Strategies of Racial Protest in Mississippi," *Journal of Southern History* 55, no. 2 (1989): 217–44. See also William H. Lawson, "No Small Thing: A Rhetorical Analysis of the 1963 Freedom Vote" (PhD diss., Florida State University, 2008).

26. For Henry's memoir, see Aaron Henry and Constance Curry, *Aaron Henry: The Fire Ever Burning* (Jackson: University Press of Mississippi, 2000). See also Minion K. C. Morrison, *Aaron Henry of Mississippi: Inside Agitator* (Fayetteville: University of Arkansas Press, 2015).

27. Taylor Branch erroneously claims that "someone loosened the lug nuts on his tires," which lead to the near-fatal head-on collision on June 18, 1963, in Jackson; see Branch, *Pillar of Fire: America in the King Years 1963–65* (New York: Simon & Schuster, 1998), 121. Whether King and fellow Tougaloo College activist John Salter were in an "accident," or whether the car crash was orchestrated by a member of the local Citizens' Council, the men's car had not been tampered with. For more on King's work in Mississippi see Edwin King and Trent Watts, *Ed King's Mississippi: Behind the Scenes of Freedom Summer* (Jackson: University Press of Mississippi, 2014); and Davis W. Houck, "Ed King's Jaw—Or, Reading, Writing, and Embodying Civil Rights," *Rhetoric & Public Affairs* 7, no. 1 (2004): 67–90.

28. Robert Moses and Charles E. Cobb Jr., *Radical Equations: Math Literacy and Civil Rights* (Boston: Beacon, 2001), 72–73.

29. The Henry/King platform called for the abolition of segregation, in housing, businesses, and schools; the ticket demanded easier access to the ballot, one in which reluctant registrars would be immediately arrested for blocking would-be Black registrants; voters for the Freedom Ticket would also support small farm loan programs, progressive taxation on large plantations, and public works projects to create badly needed infrastructure such as sewer, water, and roads, and a minimum wage of $1.25 ($10.47 in 2020 dollars); teachers would have academic freedom so that getting fired for being a member of the NAACP would be illegal; the state-funded Sovereignty Commission would be abolished, and no

state dollars would be allocated to the White Citizens' Councils. That COFO was deadly serious about its progressive campaign is also reflected in detailed budgets, plans for television advertisements, and near-constant speechmaking by Henry and King.

30. See, for example, the online newspaper archives at http://stanforddailyarchive.com/ and http://web.library.yale.edu/digital-collections/yale-daily-news-historical-archive. Both campus newspapers covered the exploits of their students extensively.

31. I conducted phone interviews in May 2020 with Stanford alumni Holt Ruffin, Frank Dubofsky, and Fowler "Skip" Martin, as well as former dean Dwight Clark. Each shared stories from that fall; it was clear that Allard Lowenstein's influence—he'd been an assistant dean on campus during the 1961–62 academic year, taking up residence in Stern Hall—was very important in their involvement with the Freedom Vote campaign. Accompanying Ruffin and Dubofsky on their travels to Mississippi was Dennis Sweeney, who'd actually spent time with Lowenstein in Jackson, during the summer of 1963. Sweeney's influence among Stanford undergraduate men was considerable, and his intimate proximity to Lowenstein was the envy of campus political life. On March 14, 1980, suffering from acute mental illness, Sweeney emptied a revolver into Lowenstein's chest in Lowenstein's New York City law office, killing him. For a detailed look at Sweeney's activism and his complicated relationship with Lowenstein, see David Harris, *Dreams Die Hard: Three Men's Journey Through the Sixties* (New York: St. Martin's Press, 1982).

32. "Stanford and the Mock Vote: What Does It Mean?," *Stanford Daily*, November 8, 1963, 2. In a lengthy personal letter, shared with me, that Martin sent to Strelitz, dated October 31, 1964, he expressed frustration with the *Daily*'s coverage of white Stanford students and Black Mississippians. He had been one of its facilitators and purveyors with Strelitz for more than a year, and some of his invective is decidedly personal: "I am really upset personally by the dual standard our efforts toward the Freedom movement are run on here, yet I know practically there can be no other way. When a Stanford student gets beaten or thrown in jail within a few hours half the Justice Department has been aroused at 4 in the morning, money is being raised, and people in general are running around like chickens with their heads cut off. Then we get word that another group of negroes or out of state workers has been thrown in jail and . . . everyone shakes their head and says what a horrible thing it is and how no one looks after the Mississippi negro, etc. etc. ad nauseum."

33. Ilene H. Strelitz, "Mock Vote Takes Turn for the Better; Stanford Contributions Are Received," *Stanford Daily*, October 31, 1963, 1.

34. Nothing in his memoir suggests he was physically there, either; see John N. Herbers, with Anne Farris Rosen, *Deep South Dispatch: Memoir of a Civil Rights Journalist* (Jackson: University Press of Mississippi, 2018).

35. Steven Schatzow, "First Group of Students Head to Mississippi to Begin Canvassing for Protest Election," *Yale Daily News*, October 18, 1963, 1, 2.

36. Jon M. Van Dyke, "Mississippi Governor, Negro Leader Voice Opinions in 'News' Interview," *Yale Daily News*, October 23, 1963, 1.

37. James Adams, "Two Yale Students Arrested in Mississippi Rights Drive," *Yale Daily News*, October 23, 1963, 1.

38. The full oral history can be viewed here: https://www.mynhtv.com/civilrights.

39. Nelson A. Soltman and Jon M. Van Dyke, "Yale in Mississippi: Is It Worthwhile?," *Yale Daily News*, October 29, 1963, 1, 2.

40. Quoted in Laura Visser-Maessen, *Robert Parris Moses: A Life in Civil Rights and Leadership at the Grassroots* (Chapel Hill: University of North Carolina Press, 2016), 164.

41. Two very different accounts of that event are offered in Sinsheimer, "The Freedom Vote of 1963," 237; and James Forman, *The Making of Black Revolutionaries* (Seattle: University of Washington Press, 1997), 357.

42. Jon M. Van Dyke, "Mississippi Negroes Seen as Near Slaves to White Landowners," *Yale Daily News*, October 23, 1963, 2.

43. Jon M. Van Dyke, "Students Trade Stories of Adventures Over Sherry at Ezra Stiles Meeting," *Yale Daily News*, November 11, 1963, 1.

44. Van Dyke, "Students Trade Stories," 3.

45. The Freedom Vote celebration was captured by Alan Ribback/Moses Moon on audiotape. His remarkable sonic archive of the movement is available at the Smithsonian's National Museum of American History and contains more than eighty hours of the movement's sounds from local meetings held between 1963 and 1964, in outposts such as Danville, Virginia, Hattiesburg and Greenwood, Mississippi, and Selma, Alabama. A guide to the collection is available online at http://sova.si.edu/record/NMAH.AC.0556. Transcriptions of select speeches, conducted by Furman University students, can be furnished upon request.

46. Mississippi, and much of the Deep South, was a one-party state, by dint of the Civil War and Reconstruction's legacy. That is, the party of Lincoln and Radical Reconstruction would not find a receptive home in Mississippi until 1964, when President Johnson's progressive civil rights legislation—most notably the 1964 Civil Rights Act—led many Democrats to switch parties.

47. See, for example, John Herbers, "50 Yale Men Aid Mississippi Negro," *New York Times*, October 30, 1963, 24; Herbers, "Norman Thomas Mocks Mississippi," *New York Times*, November 1, 1963, 22; Herbers, "Vote Drive Planned to Register 80,000 Negroes in Mississippi," *New York Times*, November 7, 1963, 30.

48. Dittmer, *Local People*, 207.

49. Dittmer, *Local People*, 207, ellipses in original. See also Eric Burner, *And Gently He Shall Lead Them: Robert Parris Moses and Civil Rights in Mississippi* (New York: New York University Press, 1994), 126.

50. James P. Marshall, *Student Activism and Civil Rights in Mississippi: Protest Politics and the Struggle for Racial Justice, 1960–1965* (Baton Rouge: Louisiana State University Press, 2013), 71.

51. Herbers, "50 Yale Men Aid Mississippi Negro," 24.

52. Marshall, *Student Activism and Civil Rights in Mississippi*, 71.

53. Papers of the Student Nonviolent Coordinating Committee, reel 39.

54. Stokely Carmichael and Ekwueme Michael Thelwell, *Ready for Revolution: The Life and Struggles of Stokely Carmichael (Kwame Ture)* (New York: Scribners, 2003), 353.

55. Carmichael and Thelwell, *Ready for Revolution*, 353–54.

56. Clayborne Carson notes, for example, that part of the success of the Freedom Vote was based on "the small number of incidents of violence directed against civil rights

workers." See Carson, *In Struggle: SNCC and the Black Awakening of the 1960s* (Cambridge, MA: Harvard University Press, 1981), 98. Similarly, Nicholas Mills notes that "with the media on hand to report what was happening to the students, the violence remained limited." See Mills, *Like a Holy Crusade: Mississippi 1964—The Turning of the Civil Rights Movement in America* (Chicago: Ivan R. Dee, 1992), 55.

57. Chafe, *Never Stop Running*, 184–85.

58. Dittmer, *Local People*, 203.

59. Hogan, *Many Minds, One Heart*, 147–48.

60. Sinsheimer, "The 1963 Freedom Vote," 232.

61. Howell Raines, *My Soul Is Rested: The Story of the Civil Rights Movement in the Deep South* (New York: Penguin, 1977), 287.

62. Visser-Maessen, *Robert Parris Moses*, 166.

63. Joseph Sinsheimer, interview by George Greene, September 16, 1978, Joseph A. Sinsheimer Papers, Duke University, Durham, NC.

64. Ken Klotz, letter to Senator Birch Bayh, October 28, 1963, Papers of the Congress of Racial Equality, reel 40.

65. Papers of the Student Nonviolent Coordinating Committee, reel 38.

66. "Over 70,000 Cast Freedom Ballots," *Student Voice* (Atlanta, Ga.), November 11, 1963, 1, https://content.wisconsinhistory.org/digital/collection/p15932coll2/id/50136/.

67. Mills, *Like a Holy Crusade*, 57.

68. Mills, *Like a Holy Crusade*, 64.

69. August Meier and Elliott Rudwick, *CORE: A Study in the Civil Rights Movement* (New York: Oxford University Press, 1973), 289.

70. Hogan, *Many Minds, One Heart*, 153.

71. James F. Findlay Jr., *Church People in the Struggle: The National Council of Churches and the Black Freedom Struggle, 1950–1970* (New York: Oxford University Press, 1992), 82–83; Visser-Maessen, *Robert Parris Moses*, 181.

72. Howard Zinn, *SNCC: The New Abolitionists* (Cambridge, MA: South End Press, 2002), 147–66.

73. Dittmer, *Local People*, 220.

74. Papers of the Student Nonviolent Coordinating Committee, reel 3, Meeting Minutes, January 23, 1964, Hattiesburg, MS. While several SNCC staff members openly supported the Summer Project, many still opposed the idea—both on philosophical grounds as well as logistical ones.

75. Payne notes that the manner in which Moses "forced the issue was a long-term source of anger within COFO precisely because it was the opposite of SNCC's usual consensual style." Payne, *I've Got The Light of Freedom*, 473n21.

76. CBS did an investigation into Louis Allen's murder on an episode of *60 Minutes* that aired in April 2011; see http://www.cbsnews.com/news/cold-case-the-murder-of-louis-allen-15-04-2011/.

77. Payne, *I've Got the Light of Freedom*, 300.

78. Moses and Cobb, *Radical Equations*, 76.

79. Quoted in Raines, *My Soul Is Rested*, 274.

80. Mills, *Like A Holy Crusade*, 84, emphasis in original.

81. Payne, *I've Got the Light of Freedom*, 300.

82. Claude Sitton, "Negroes to Spur Mississippi Drive," *New York Times*, March 16, 1964, 26.

83. Dave Dennis, letter to James T. McCain, May 27, 1964, Papers of the Congress of Racial Equality, reel 39. Seth Cagin and Philip Dray claim that Schwerner had requested to CORE officials that Chaney be promoted to paid staff in April 1964; see Cagin and Dray, *We Are Not Afraid: The Story of Goodman, Schwerner, and Chaney, and the Civil Rights Campaign for Mississippi* (New York: Scribner, 1988), 271.

84. Carol V. R. George, *One Mississippi, Two Mississippi: Methodists, Murder, and the Struggle for Racial Justice in Neshoba County* (New York: Oxford University Press, 2015), 125.

85. George, *One Mississippi, Two Mississippi*, 127.

86. Don Whitehead, *Attack on Terror: The FBI Against the Ku Klux Klan in Mississippi* (New York: Funk & Wagnalls, 1970), 22.

87. Whitehead, *Attack on Terror*, 23.

88. Whitehead, *Attack on Terror*, 26.

89. COFO had taken brief notice of Boyd's suspension in a news digest from April; in an item headed "Alcorn Followup," the authors quoted directly from Boyd's letter. SNCC, in particular, may have had its eye on Alcorn not just because it was a state HBCU, but also for possible recruitment purposes. Leaders in SNCC surely knew that the recently slain Mississippi NAACP leader Medgar Evers, as well as his combative wife, Myrlie, were Alcorn students. Papers of the Student Nonviolent Coordinating Committee, reel 39.

90. The full text and audio of the address is available at http://americanradioworks.publicradio.org/features/Blackspeech/bmoses.html.

91. In his otherwise excellent book about Freedom Summer, Bruce Watson erroneously claims that Goodman's recruitment into the Summer Project was facilitated by a speech at Queens College delivered by Fannie Lou Hamer. According to research conducted by Mark Levy, a Queens alumnus and a Summer Project veteran, Hamer did not speak at the college in the spring of 1964. See Bruce Watson, *Freedom Summer: The Savage Season That Made Mississippi Burn and Made America a Democracy* (New York: Viking, 2010), 83. Email correspondence with Mark Levy, December 14, 2010. More recent versions of the book have corrected the error. Goodman's matriculation as an anthropology student at Queens is intriguing given that the founder of the program was Hortense Powdermaker, whose book *After Freedom: A Cultural Study in the Deep South* was based on fieldwork conducted in Indianola, Mississippi, in 1932 and 1933. Whether Goodman was Powdermaker's student at Queens, or whether he'd read her foundational text on race relations in the Delta, isn't known. But departmental representatives at Queens indicate the possibility is "highly likely" that Goodman was Powdermaker's student.

92. In a May "Memo to Accepted Applicants," volunteers were advised by COFO: "We hope you are making preparations to have bond money ready in the event of your arrest. Bond money for a single arrest usually runs around $500." Papers of the Student Nonviolent Coordinating Committee, reel 39.

93. Papers of the Student Nonviolent Coordinating Committee, reel 39.

94. Papers of the Student Nonviolent Coordinating Committee, reel 39.

95. See letter of April 27, 1964, Papers of the Student Nonviolent Coordinating Committee, reel 39.

96. Letter of April 27, 1964, Papers of the Student Nonviolent Coordinating Committee, reel 39.

97. "Att. Gen. Joe Patterson Speaks Here on Race, Communism and Freedom," *Franklin Advocate* (Meadville, MS), March 19, 1964, 1.

98. For more on the Bunkley Klavern, see MacLean, *The Past Is Never Dead*, 31–32. Many of the Bunkley Klansmen worshiped at the Bunkley Baptist Church; in fact, Charles Marcus Edwards was a deacon at the church at the time of the investigation into the murders of Moore and Dee in 2005.

99. David Webb, "Pre-Dawn Explosion Partially Destroys Bude Café; Officers Are Investigating," *Franklin Advocate*, April 9, 1964, 1.

100. Details about the kidnapping and murder of Moore and Dee come principally from four sources: MacLean, *The Past Is Never Dead*; Alston and Dickerson, *Devil's Sanctuary*; David Ridgen's documentary film *Mississippi Cold Case*; and the very important court documents filed as part of Seale's appeal of his conviction, available at http://www.justice.gov/sites/default/files/crt/legacy/2010/12/14/seale_decision.pdf.

101. Special Report, May 1, 1964, Erle Johnston to Paul Johnson Jr., Sovereignty Commission Papers, Box 135, Folder 9, University of Southern Mississippi, Hattiesburg, MS. The irony, of course, was palpable: the Klan and APWR were bringing weapons into the state even as they murdered Moore and Dee for suspicions of the same.

102. Aaron Henry, Robert Moses, and Dave Dennis, letter to President Lyndon Johnson, May 25, 1964, Papers of the Student Nonviolent Coordinating Committee, reel 14.

103. Claude Sitton, "Mississippi Is Gripped by Fear of Violence in Civil Rights Drive," *New York Times*, May 30, 1964, 1.

104. Hedrick Smith, "President Watches Race Outlook Here with Some Concern," *New York Times*, June 5, 1964, 1.

105. Quoted in Visser-Maessen, *Robert Parris Moses*, 191.

106. Lisa Anderson Todd, *For a Voice and the Vote: My Journey with the Mississippi Freedom Democratic Party* (Lexington: University of Kentucky Press, 2014), 92.

107. Dr. Harold Taylor, letter to President Lyndon Johnson, June 11, 1964, Papers of the Student Nonviolent Coordinating Committee, reel 39.

108. At a late hour, the president and Board of Trustees of Berea College backed out of a commitment given to the National Council of Churches that the college would host the two-week COFO training sessions. The Presbyterian-aligned Western College for Women, though, quickly signed on. See Findlay, *Church People in the Struggle*, 85.

109. Robert Moses, letter to Summer Project Volunteers, June 11, 1964, Papers of the Student Nonviolent Coordinating Committee, reel 39.

110. The quotes are taken from the Howard Zinn Freedom Summer papers housed digitally at the Wisconsin Historical Society. See https://content.wisconsinhistory.org/digital/collection/p15932coll2/id/11771/rec/1.

111. Claude Sitton, "Students Briefed on Peril in South," *New York Times*, June 17, 1964, 18.

112. Sitton, "Novices Irk 'Pros' in Rights Course," *New York Times*, June 18, 1964, 25.

113. Robert Moses, letter to President Lyndon Johnson, June 14, 1964, Papers of the Student Nonviolent Coordinating Committee, reel 39.

114. Carmichael and Thelwell, *Ready for Revolution*, 368.

115. Quoted in *Freedom on My Mind*, directed by Marilyn Mulford and Connie Field (Berkeley, CA: Clarity Films, 1994).

116. Quoted in Visser-Maessen, *Robert Parris Moses*, 203.

117. Claude Sitton, "U.S. Official Warns Mississippi-Bound Students," *New York Times*, June 20, 1964, 12.

118. Carmichael and Thelwell, *Ready for Revolution*, 370.

119. Carmichael and Thelwell, *Ready for Revolution*, 371.

120. "Mississippi Tense over Voter Drive," *New York Times*, June 21, 1964, 64.

121. Quoted in Gene Roberts and Hank Klibanoff, *The Race Beat: The Press, The Civil Rights Struggle, and the Awakening of a Nation* (New York: Knopf, 2007), 354.

122. "Localisms ... by Lewis," editorial, *Woodville Republican*, July 3, 1964, 1.

123. "The Long Summer Begins," editorial, *Jackson Advocate*, July 11, 1964.

124. Grady McAlexander, "Short Casts," *South Reporter* (Holly Springs, MS), August 6, 1964, 1.

125. "Dave's Webb," *Franklin Advocate*, July 9, 1964, 1.

126. "No Room Here for Communists," editorial, *South Reporter*, July 30, 1964, 1.

127. "It's Time to Be Calm and Cool-Headed," editorial, *Neshoba Democrat*, June 25, 1964, 4.

128. "A Challenge for Leflore County," editorial, *Greenwood Commonwealth*, June 22, 1964, 1.

129. "With Dignity and Restraint," editorial, *Greenwood Commonwealth*, June 22, 1964, 6.

130. "The People and the Intruders," editorial, *Clarksdale Press Register*, June 24, 1964, 7.

131. "City Meddler," editorial, *Enterprise-Tocsin* (Indianola, MS), July 2, 1964, 1.

132. "Time to Wait," editorial, *Delta Democrat-Times*, July 19, 1964, 4.

133. "Changes in Mississippi," editorial, *Delta Democrat-Times*, July 21, 1964, 4.

134. As chairman of the powerful Senate Judiciary Committee, Eastland could hold hostage nearly all civil rights legislation proposed in the Senate. For a fascinating account of how Johnson and his allies made an end run around Eastland's committee, which would lead to the Civil Rights Act of 1964, see Robert A. Caro, *The Passage of Power: The Years of Lyndon Johnson* (New York: Knopf, 2012), 430–569.

135. Whitehead, *Attack on Terror*, 4–9.

136. William Bradford Huie, *Three Lives For Mississippi* (New York: WCC, 1965), 106–7.

137. Whitehead, *Attack on Terror*, 9.

138. Dittmer, *Local People*, 247.

139. Robert Penn Warren, *Who Speaks for the Negro?* (New York: Vintage, 1965), 124.

140. Visser-Maessen, *Robert Parris Moses*, 207.

141. In addition to SNCC's detailed log of events in the hours and days following the disappearance, the best sourcing on the Goodman-Schwerner-Chaney narrative is Dittmer's *Local People*, Huie's *Three Lives For Mississippi*, and Cagin and Dray's *We Are Not Afraid*. See Incident Report, Papers of the Student Nonviolent Coordinating Committee, reel 39.

142. Rev. Clay F. Lee had just finished preaching only his third sermon at First United Methodist. Later, in December 1964, Lee would deliver a memorable sermon, indirectly about the community's involvement in the murders, titled "Herod Is in Christmas." That sermon would be the focus of an archival search recorded by the *New York Times* in 2013; see Samuel G. Freedman, "Civil Rights Sermon Is Mislaid, but Not Forgotten, *New York Times*, March 7, 2013.

143. But, in COFO's detailed logs, a call to the Neshoba County Jail was recorded for 5:30 p.m., just an hour after they'd been booked into the jail. Someone, never identified, said the men were not being held there.

144. On May 29, 1964, just three weeks earlier, Rev. Ed King and four colleagues, Eli Hochstedler, Joan Trumpauer, Hamid Kizilbash, and his wife, Jeannette, had been forced off the road by Klansmen near Canton after an evening voter registration event held at Wesley Methodist Church. As King relates the story, everyone in the car understood that they were likely going to die at the hands of the Klan. As they awaited execution, though, King was able to begin a halting dialogue with one of the mob's leaders (their driver, Kizilbash, was Pakistani, not Black, and could provoke an international incident if killed); the mob eventually, reluctantly, allowed them to go. At Oxford, during the training sessions, King claims that such strategy and tactics, rooted in Gandhian principles, were discussed. The premise was profoundly humanizing: even the most vile Klansman could potentially be reached. Interestingly, in the Sovereignty Commission Papers at the University of Southern Mississippi, Kizilbash's letter of June 2, 1964, to Governor Paul Johnson documents that evening's terrorism and encourages him to "take some action to prevent such violence"; see Sovereignty Commission Papers, Box 135, Folder 10. Kizilbash was assistant professor at Tougaloo College's Social Science Division.

145. Roberts and Klibanoff, *The Race Beat*, 359.

146. Claude Sitton, "3 in Rights Drive Reported Missing," *New York Times*, June 23, 1964, 1.

147. http://web2.millercenter.org/lbj/audiovisual/whrecordings/telephone/conversations/1964/lbj_wh6406_14_3836.mp3.

148. Quoted in *American Experience: Freedom Summer*, directed by Stanley Nelson (Arlington, VA: Public Broadcasting Service, 2014). The segment can be viewed at https://www.youtube.com/watch?v=_2ssdtB-sAI.

149. Quoted in Len Holt, *The Summer That Didn't End: The Story of the Mississippi Civil Rights Project of 1964* (New York: Da Capo, 1965), 30.

150. Quoted in Nelson, *Freedom Summer*, https://www.youtube.com/watch?v=_2ssdtB-sAI.

151. Watson, *Freedom Summer*, 93.

152. Nick Kotz, *Judgment Days: Lyndon Baines Johnson, Martin Luther King Jr., and the Laws That Changed America* (Boston: Mariner, 2005), 172.

153. For two accounts of the search for the three men, see Carmichael and Thelwell, *Ready for Revolution*, 374–81; and Cleveland Sellers with Robert Terrell, *The River of No Return: The Autobiography of a Black Militant and the Life and Death of SNCC* (Jackson: University Press of Mississippi, 1990), 81–93.

154. "Our Purpose Must Be Unmistakably Clear," editorial, *Vicksburg Evening-Post*, August 6, 1964, 4.

155. "Localisms . . . by Lewis," *Woodville Republican*, July 3, 1964, 1.

156. Report from Colonel Al Lingo to J. A. Gordon, June 25, 1964, Box 135, Folder 10, Sovereignty Commission Papers, University of Southern Mississippi, Hattiesburg, MS.

157. Raines, *My Soul Is Rested*, 288.

158. Elizabeth Martinez, ed., *Letters from Mississippi* (Brookline, MA: Zephyr, 2007), 157.

159. Typical of such claims was the *New York Times*'s lede on November 8, 1964, announcing the arrest of Klansmen James Ford Seale and Charles Marcus Edwards. Moore's and Dee's "bodies were found by chance during the search for the three civil rights workers." "2 Whites Seized in Negro Slayings," *New York Times*, November 7, 1964, 56.

160. Donna Ladd, "Fighting Back in Klan Nation," *Jackson Free Press*, March 21, 2007, http://www.jacksonfreepress.com/news/2007/mar/21/fighting-back-in-klan-nation/.

161. Donna Ladd, "Franklin County Editors, Past and Present," *Jackson Free Press*, June 8, 2007, http://www.jacksonfreepress.com/news/2007/jun/08/day-8-franklin-county -editors-past-and-present/.

162. James F. Seale, "People Should Fight Communist Menace . . . Obey God's Law First and Foremost," *Franklin Advocate*, July 23, 1964, 7 (ellipsis in original).

163. "Dave's Webb," *Franklin Advocate*, July 9, 1964, 1.

164. Maryanne Vollers, for example, argues that "their [Moore's and Dee's] disappearance would have probably gone unnoticed under different circumstances—just two more local boys gone missing, never to be found." See Vollers, *Ghosts of Mississippi: The Murder of Medgar Evers, the Trials of Byron De La Beckwith, and the Haunting of the New South* (Boston: Little Brown, 1995), 220.

165. "River Yields Second Body," *Clarion Ledger* (Jackson, MS), July 14, 1964, 1.

166. "Second Mutilated Body Found in River Offshoot," *Hattiesburg American*, July 13, 1964, 1.

167. "College President Identifies Body; CR Trio Ruled Out," *Delta Democrat-Times*, July 13, 1964, 1.

168. "Two Slayings Apparently Unreported," *Greenwood Commonwealth*, July 14, 1964, 1.

169. "Fisherman Finds Body in Louisiana," *New York Times*, July 13, 1964, 13.

170. John Herbers, "Negro's Death Mystifies Mother in Mississippi," *New York Times*, July 15, 1964, 17.

171. For the full telephone conversation between Johnson and Hoover, see http://web2. millercenter.org/lbj/audiovisual/whrecordings/telephone/conversations/1964/lbj_wh6407 _07_4221.mp3.

172. Filmmaker David Ridgen notes a similar effect; see Shaila Dewan, "Push to Resolve Fading Killings of Rights Era," *New York Times*, February 3, 2007, A11.

173. Letter of Roy Torkington, July 15, 1964, Folder 1, Torkington Freedom Summer Collection, University of Southern Mississippi, Hattiesburg, MS.

174. Quoted in Martinez, *Letters from Mississippi*, 215–15; and Watson, *Freedom Summer*, 147.

175. Phil Ochs, "Here's to the State of Mississippi," 1965.

176. Matt Jones, "In the Mississippi River," 1964.

177. In her otherwise exemplary history, Visser-Maessen erroneously claims that Moore and Dee had been "missing since 1963," and that both men were "Alcorn student-activists." See Visser-Maessen, *Robert Parris Moses*, 210.

178. Quoted in Don Mitchell, *The Freedom Summer Murders* (New York: Scholastic, 2014), 133.

179. Fannie Lou Hamer, foreword to *Stranger at the Gates: A Summer in Mississippi*, by Tracy Sugarman (New York: Hill and Wang, 1966), viii.

180. Marco Williams, *Freedom Summer* (Los Angeles: A&E Television Networks, 2006).

181. Gill died on July 26, 2007, at the age of fifty-nine, from arterial sclerosis. An unreturned email from a stranger, of course, isn't terribly remarkable, but it did fuel my curiosity.

182. Dittmer, *Local People*, 251–52.

183. In a lightly redacted report sent to the Southern Poverty Law Center, the Federal Bureau of Investigation includes more than thirty-five pages of documents germane to the Orsby case. The FBI concluded that Orsby's death was caused by accidental drowning. They closed the case on April 12, 2010. See https://www.justice.gov/crt/case-document/herbert -orsby. I am in possession of the report issued to the SPLC.

184. Cagin and Dray, *We Are Not Afraid*, 371–72.

185. For Black newspapers that covered the mysterious death of Herbert Orsby, see "Body of Teenager Found in Big Black River Miss.," *St. Louis Argus*, September 18, 1964, 1; "Body of Boy, 14, Found in Mississippi," *Call and Post* (Cleveland, OH), September 19, 1964, 7b; "Death of Teen in Miss. Is Called an Accident," *Chicago Defender*, September 12, 1964, 4; "CORE Youth's Body Found; Dynamiters Bomb 2 Buildings," *Florida Star* (Jacksonville), September 12, 1964, 1; "Probe Drowning of CORE Youth," *Florida Star*, September 19, 1964, 8; "CORE Youths Death Spurs FBI Probe," *Indianapolis Recorder*, September 12, 1964, 2; "Discovery Dead Boy's Body After Weeks Harassment," *Pittsburgh Courier*, September 19, 1964, 1; "Drowning of Boy, 14, in Miss. Ruled Accident," *Afro-American* (Baltimore), September 15, 1964, 12; and "Probe Drowning of CORE Youth," *Michigan Chronicle*, September 19, 1964, 6A. The white press also covered the Orsby death; see "Orleans Youth Found in River," *Times-Picayune* (New Orleans), September 10, 1964, 1; "Death of Youth Said Accidental," *Times-Picayune*, September 11, 1964, 1; "Negro Boy's Death Ruled Accident," *Memphis Commercial Appeal*, September 10, 1964, 16; "Body of Negro Boy Is Found in State River," *Jackson Daily News*, September 10, 1964, 2b; and "Negro Youth Drowned in Big Black River," *Lexington Advertiser*, September 17, 1964, 8.

As in the Moore and Dee case, the FBI moved in immediately to investigate Orsby's suspicious death; in fact, their report, obtained through a Freedom of Information Act request by the Southern Poverty Law Center (SPLC), indicates that Burke Marshall, the assistant attorney general for civil rights, personally ordered the investigation, and agents' reports frequently were sent to FBI associate director Clyde Tolson in Washington, DC—a close confidante of J. Edgar Hoover. In a word, his death was taken very seriously as a possible civil rights case. The FBI's report, which features many redacted documents, strongly suggests that Orsby's death was in fact an accidental drowning. The fourteen-year-old boy from New Orleans, visiting his grandparents in Pickens, left their house on Monday,

September 7. His body was discovered on a snag of logs in the Big Black River on Wednesday morning, September 9, after he was reported missing. His grandfather, Tobe Hart, did not say that Orsby was wearing a CORE T-shirt, despite persistent rumors that he had been wearing such a shirt; in fact, in one document, Hart claims that Orsby's clothes had no identifying documents other than a laundromat mark. Reports by the coroner and chief of police did not indicate any bodily trauma suggestive of violence; moreover, the Pickens community was not involved in Freedom Summer and was nearly twenty miles north and east of Canton, where CORE had an ongoing and highly successful project. Nevertheless, Orsby, often wrongly identified in official documents as Hubert Oarsby, is included among the SPLC's National Civil Rights Memorial Center's seventy-four "Forgotten" victims; see https://www.splcenter.org/what-we-do/civil-rights-memorial/forgotten.

In attempting to learn more about Herbert Orsby and whether he was involved with CORE, in Mississippi or his hometown of New Orleans, which had a very effective and highly organized office, I first contacted Jarvis DeBerry, a journalist at the *Times-Picayune*. DeBerry put me in touch with Jerome Smith, a leading organizer in CORE's New Orleans office, who also still lives there. We spoke by telephone in February 2012, several days after he'd learned of my search for information on Orsby. He reported that none of his contacts knew of him, that nobody knew of a teenager killed wearing a CORE T-shirt, and that he very likely was not involved with any civil rights activity. FBI documents indicate that Orsby was buried on Friday, September 11, 1964, in the cemetery of Cypress Grove Baptist Church, west of Pickens. Despite an extensive search, I could not locate his grave. A brother, Roy, survives Herbert and apparently lives in New Orleans; see Dan Barry, Campbell Robertson, and Robbie Brown, "When Cold Cases Stay Cold," *New York Times*, March 16, 2013, http://www.nytimes.com/2013/03/17/us/souths-cold-cases-reopened-but -still-unresolved.html?_r=0.

186. Vollers, *Ghosts of Mississippi*, 220. Vollers's book was the basis of the 1996 Hollywood film by the same name.

187. Huie paid the accused murderers of Emmett Till, Roy Bryant, and J. W. Milam more than $3,000 to get the "true story" of what supposedly happened. Huie's account, published in the January 24, 1956, edition of *Look* magazine, was a blockbuster. Perhaps more importantly, for the better part of fifty years, the so-called confession offered by the murderers functioned rhetorically as the truth of what supposedly happened in the early morning hours of August 28, 1955. Thanks to the intrepid work of filmmaker Keith Beauchamp and several others, we know that almost nothing in the *Look* confession was true; instead, Milam and Bryant offered a series of concocted events that celebrated their roles as preserving white womanhood in the wake of the unanimous *Brown* Supreme Court decision—and made Emmett Till out to be a marauding Black man intent on having his way sexually with white women. In writing the confession, Huie conveniently overlooked the courtroom testimony of Willie Reed, a local Black eyewitness, who saw a truck driven by Milam, with at least seven people in it, pull into a shed near Drew. Reed identified Till in the bed of the truck and later heard his screams as he was tortured and murdered. For a fascinating archival account of the *Look* article, see Dave Tell, "'The Shocking Story' of Emmett Till and the Politics of Public Confession," *Quarterly Journal of Speech* 94, no. 2

(2008): 154–76; and Dave Tell, *Confessional Crises and Cultural Politics in Twentieth Century America* (University Park: Pennsylvania State University Press, 2013), 63–90. For the best historical account of the Till case, see Devery S. Anderson, *Emmett Till: The Murder That Shocked the World and Propelled the Civil Rights Movement* (Jackson: University Press of Mississippi, 2015).

188. Huie, *Three Lives For Mississippi.*

189. William McCord, *Mississippi: The Long Hot Summer* (New York: W. W. Norton, 1965). McCord described himself as a "minor participant" in the events of Freedom Summer and disclaimed efforts at "scholarly objectivity."

190. A July 12 entry with the location "Jackson" reads: "Half-body found in Mississippi identified as Charles Moore, former Alcorn A&M student. Second half-body found in river"; see Len Holt, *The Summer That Didn't End*, 216. Herbert Orsby's body is not recorded, perhaps because the Summer Project was deemed over by early September. The last entry for the "Running Summary of Incidents" is dated August 26. After Freedom Summer concluded, on September 9, at 2:20 p.m., COFO's WATS Line reporter, E. Simpson, recorded the "rumor" that a body wearing a CORE shirt had been "pulled out of a river." Later that same day, Peggy Sharp noted in her WATS report that "Henry Orsby's" body had been recovered from the Big Black River; see https://content.wisconsinhistory.org/digital/collection/p15932coll2/id/47445/rec/1.

191. The entire issue of *Ramparts* is in the Mississippi Sovereignty Commission papers and can be located at https://dickatlee.com/issues/mississippi/mississippi_eyewitness/index.html.

192. Holt, *The Summer That Didn't End*; Martinez, *Letters from Mississippi*. The July 16 letter from Tchula, quoted above, mentions the bodies that would later be identified as Moore and Dee.

193. Whitehead, *Attack on Terror.*

194. James Farmer, *Lay Bare the Heart: An Autobiography of the Civil Rights Movement* (Fort Worth: Texas Christian University Press, 1985); Carmichael and Thelwell, *Ready for Revolution*; and Sellers, *River of No Return.*

195. Unita Blackwell with JoAnne Prichard Morris, *Barefootin': Life Lessons from the Road to Freedom* (New York: Crown, 2006), 94.

196. Sally Belfrage, preface to *Freedom Summer* (Charlottesville: University of Virginia Press, 1990), xv.

197. Moses's remarks can be found online at http://www.crmvet.org/info/mosesq.htm.

198. Access to all of the Eyes on the Price Oral History archive is available at http://digital.wustl.edu/eyesontheprize/.

199. *Eyes on the Prize*, directed by Henry Hampton (Boston: Blackside Films, 1986).

200. The online Teacher's Guide states, "In 1963, Black citizens of Mississippi had been disenfranchised for years. Earlier attempts to register to vote had been met with intimidation and reprisals. As more efforts were made to register voters, the state decided to withhold food and other aid from poor rural areas, which was especially devastating to the Black community during a difficult winter. The arrival of popular comedian Dick Gregory with a plane full of supplies brought media attention and public scrutiny. The resulting

publicity helped spark the idea for what would become known as 'Freedom Summer'";
see https://tn.pbslearningmedia.org/resource/amex26.soc.fscatalyst/freedomsummerthe
catalyst/. While publicity certainly accompanied Gregory's generous effort, his work had
absolutely nothing to do with the development of the ideas that would lead to Freedom
Summer. On the other hand, and as countless movement activists and historians have
noted, the Freedom Vote of October and November 1963 led directly to it.

201. "Murder in Mississippi," website for PBS's *American Experience*, http://www.pbs
.org/wgbh/americanexperience/features/general-article/freedomsummer-murder/. On the
same website, under the "Timeline: Freedom Summer" tab, the following is written: "The
FBI opens its first Mississippi field office in Jackson. In the coming days, more than 200
FBI agents will join the search for Chaney, Schwerner and Goodman, whom investigators
believe crossed state lines. Agents combed through 10 counties and recovered the bodies of
eight other Black men during their search."

202. Ives, *American Experience: 1964*.

203. Carla Murphy, "Remembering Freedom Summer 1964: Heather Booth," Colorlines.
com, http://www.colorlines.com/articles/remembering-freedom-summer-1964-heather
-booth. Booth has repeated the claim in oral histories, including one with Florida State
University doctoral student Christine Willingham in 2012 (transcript available upon
request).

204. Mary Elizabeth King, "How the Mississippi Freedom Summer Can Best Be
Honored," October 20, 2014, http://wagingnonviolence.org/feature/mississippi-freedom
-summer-can-best-honored/.

205. Askia Muhammad, "Still Here, Still Struggling, Still Fighting," *Final Call*, July 2,
2014, http://www.finalcall.com/artman/publish/National_News_2/article_101572.shtml.

206. George E. Curry, "Mississippi: 'I'll Go as Far as Memphis,'" *Tri-State Defender*, June
26, 2014, 4.

207. Nikole Hannah-Jones, "Freedom Summer, 1964: Did It Really Change Mississippi?,"
The Atlantic, July 8, 2014, http://www.theatlantic.com/politics/archive/2014/07/the-ghosts
-of-freedom-summer-in-greenwood-mississippi/374106/.

208. Rosalind Bentley, "Telling the Story—Charles McDew Remembers Those Who
Died For Freedom," *Star Tribune* (Minneapolis and St. Paul, MN), January 24, 1993, 1E.
Historians, too, often and erroneously fused the two very different accounts. Kotz, for example, claims, "As federal and state lawmen dragged rivers and lakes looking for the bodies
of Goodman, Chaney, and Schwerner, they found instead the bodies of three other civil
rights participants. The bodies of Charles Moore and Henry Dee, both nineteen and activists at Alcorn A&M, a Black college, were found in the Pearl River. The headless body of another Black youth, his legs tied together, was recovered in the Old River near Natchez." See
Kotz, *Judgment Days*, 172. Similarly, presidential candidate Jesse Jackson, in his now-famous
speech delivered at the 1984 Democratic Convention stated, "Twenty years ago, tears welled
up in our eyes as the bodies of Schwerner, Goodman, and Chaney were dredged from the
depths of a river in Mississippi."

209. Dave Dennis, *Jackson Advocate*, June 26, 2014, 8A. Dennis's article appears to be
identical to a speech he delivered at a fiftieth anniversary of Freedom Summer; see http://

freedom50.org/2014/07/07/2014-07-07-dave-dennis-unsung-heroes-of-1964-mississippi
-freedom-summer/.

210. Jim Dann, *Challenging the Mississippi Fire Bombers: Memories of Mississippi 1964–65* (Montreal: Baraka Books, 2013), 55.

211. Jerry Mitchell, "New Details on the FBI Paying $30K to Solve the Mississippi Burning Case," February 15, 2010, *Journey to Justice* (blog), http://blogs.clarionledger.com/jmitchell/2010/02/15/did-the-fbi-pay-30k-to-locate-the-bodies-of-the-three-missing-civil -rights-workers/.

212. Cooper's oral history can be accessed at http://ufdc.uflib.ufl.edu/AA00018126/00 001?search=chaney.

213. Matt Herron, "Photography in Difficult Times: Documenting the Civil Rights Movement," in *Freedom Is a Constant Struggle: An Anthology of the Mississippi Civil Rights Movement*, ed. Susie Erenrich (Montgomery, AL: Black Belt Press, 1999), 259.

214. Hollis Watkins and C. Liegh McInnis, *Brother Hollis: The Sankofa of a Movement Man* (Oakland, CA: Sankofa Press, 2016).

215. Watkins and McInnis, *Brother Hollis*, 231–32.

216. Civil Rights Movement Archive (website), "Lynching of Chaney, Schwerner & Goodman (June)," http://www.crmvet.org/tim/tim64b.htm#1964csg.

217. Zellner's memoir is revealing, in part, because he traveled with Rita Schwerner in the days following her husband's disappearance; see Bob Zellner with Constance Curry, *The Wrong Side of Murder Creek: A White Southerner in the Freedom Movement* (Montgomery, AL: NewSouth, 2008), 246–52. Forman, who was SNCC's executive secretary, was famously scrupulous in his documentation of the movement; his memoir, *Black Revolutionaries*, says nothing about the discovery of unnamed Black bodies during Freedom Summer. Cobb's book of civil rights sites is silent about Moore, Dee, or Orsby, nor does he say anything about Black bodies being discovered during the search for Goodman, Schwerner, and Chaney; see Charles E. Cobb Jr., *On the Road to Freedom: A Guided Tour of the Civil Rights Trail* (Chapel Hill, NC: Algonquin, 2008).

218. Florence Mars with Lynn Eden, *Witness in Philadelphia* (Baton Rouge: Louisiana State University Press, 1977), 100. Mars does get wrong the fact that Moore and Dee went missing on May 2, not April 25. A little-known but very consequential fact about Mars is that she attended the murder trial of Roy Bryant and J. W. Milam, who were accused of killing fourteen-year-old Chicagoan Emmett Till on August 28, 1955. Mars attended the trial in Sumner with her close friend Betty Pearson, who would later serve as a critically important member of the Emmett Till Memorial Commission in Tallahatchie County in the early 2000s. Mars took nearly sixty beautifully composed black-and-white photographs at the Till trial, which are archived at the Mississippi Department of Archives and History in Jackson.

219. Jaclyn Youhana, "Remembering the Movement," *Journal Gazette* (Fort Wayne, IN), May 24, 2011, 1D.

220. Janus Adams, "Lest We Forget," *The Advocate* (Stamford-Norwalk, CT), np.

221. Doug McAdam, *Freedom Summer* (New York: Oxford University Press, 1988).

222. Watson, *Freedom Summer*, 266. See also McAdam, *Freedom Summer*, 5. Martinez makes the same point in her preface, specifically mentioning Mario Savio, Heather Tobis

Booth, Pam Parker Chude Allen, and Kathie Amatniek and their work on behalf of various movements; see Martinez, *Letters from Mississippi*, xviii.

223. For Michel Foucault's critique of continuous historiography, see Foucault, *The Archaeology of Knowledge & the Discourse on Language*, trans. Alan Sheridan (New York: Pantheon, 1970).

224. The three films are *Attack on Terror: The FBI vs. the Ku Klux Klan* (1975), *Mississippi Burning* (1988), and *Murder in Mississippi* (1990). Presently, only the latter two are available commercially on DVD. *Attack on Terror* aired originally on February 20, 1975, as a two-part miniseries on CBS.

225. See George Lipsitz, *The Possessive Investment in Whiteness: How White People Profit from Identity Politics* (Philadelphia, PA: Temple University Press, 1998), 219. Madison agrees with Lipsitz that *Mississippi Burning* "probably frames memory of (the 1960s) period for the greatest number of people." Quoted in Kelly J. Madison, "Legitimation Crisis and Containment: The Anti-Racist-White-Hero Film," *Critical Studies in Mass Communication* 16, no. 4 (1999): 410.

226. *Mississippi Burning* is one of the most analyzed civil rights–themed films by rhetorical critics; see Kristen Hoerl, "Burning Mississippi into Memory? Cinematic Amnesia as a Resource for Remembering Civil Rights," *Critical Studies in Media Communication* 26, no. 1 (2009): 54–79; Madison, "Legitimation Crisis and Containment," 399–416; S. Brinson, "The Myth of White Superiority in Mississippi Burning," *Southern Communication Journal* 60, no. 3 (1995): 111–21; and H. Bourgeois, "Hollywood and the Civil Rights Movement: The Case of Mississippi Burning," *Howard Communication Journal* 4, no. 1–2 (1992): 165–71.

227. While the film accurately represents several key details in the opening car chase, including Price's 1957 Chevy and its whip antenna, the CORE Ford Fairlane station wagon, and the attempt to elude capture by making a fast right turn on County Road 492, Parker highlights the whiteness of both Goodman and Schwerner. First, Schwerner, with his trademark facial hair—he was nicknamed "Goatee" by the Klan—is driving the getaway car. Second, Andrew Goodman is in the passenger seat and the focus of several shots during the extended chase. Meanwhile, James Chaney is left as a rather bored back-seat passenger, stating laconically, "Oh, they ain't playin', you better believe it." In actuality, Chaney was driving the station wagon, Schwerner was in the passenger seat, and Goodman was in the back seat. Moreover, the one killing viewers can fleetingly glimpse is a bullet to Schwerner's head. In sum, the plot has been carefully and strategically whitened to emphasize Goodman and Schwerner at the expense of James Chaney. That Chaney is rendered marginal, at best, "is not a trivial detail," as Madison persuasively argues; see Madison, "Legitimation Crisis and Containment," 411.

228. The Memorial Committee, in fact, explicitly uses McAdam's 1988 book, *Freedom Summer*, as a source for many of the panels.

229. All of Mississippi's civil rights historical markers can be viewed at http://www.mississippimarkers.com/civil-rights.html.

230. See part of the FBI's report at https://www.justice.gov/crt/case-document/herbert-orsby.

231. Davis W. Houck and David E. Dixon, eds., *Rhetoric, Religion, and the Civil Rights Movement, 1954–1965* (Waco, TX: Baylor University Press, 2006), 776.

232. Mississippi Department of Archives and History, Lesson Five: Mississippi in 1964, A Turning Point," 2014, http://archives.usnx.com/sites/default/files/2020-03/Lesson-Five -Mississippi-in-1964-A-Turning-Point.pdf.

233. Barack Obama, "Remarks by President at Presentation of Medal of Freedom," November 24, 2014, https://www.whitehouse.gov/the-press-office/2014/11/24/remarks-pres ident-presentation-medal-freedom. Obama also made mention of the three men at a speech that April, stating, "We're at a time when we're marking many anniversaries. And it's interesting for me—I've been on this Earth 52 years, and so to see the progress we've made is to see my own life and the progression that's happened. You think about *Brown v. Board of Education*, and the Civil Rights Act, and the Voting Rights Act, and Freedom Summer. And with those anniversaries, we have new reason to remember those who made it possible for us to be here. Like the three civil rights workers in Mississippi—two white, one Black—who were murdered 50 years ago as they tried to help their fellow citizens register to vote. James Chaney and Andrew Goodman and Michael Schwerner believed so strongly that change was possible they were willing to lay down their lives for it. The least you can do is take them up on the gift that they have given you"; see "Remarks by the President at the National Action Network's 16th Annual Convention," April 11, 2014, https://www.white house.gov/the-press-office/2014/04/11/remarks-president-national-action-networks-16th -annual-convention. Obama's conflation of Freedom Summer with the three martyred men offers a revealing, and altogether unexceptional, window onto the history and memory of the Summer Project.

234. King and Watts, *Ed King's Mississippi*, 22–23.

235. For an analysis of the long versus short approaches to the civil rights movement, see Steven F. Lawson, "Freedom Then, Freedom Now: The Historiography of the Civil Rights Movement," *American Historical Review* 96, no. 2 (1991): 456–71.

236. James Baldwin, *The Evidence of Things Not Seen* (New York: Henry Holt, 1985), 99, emphasis in original.

237. See, for example, Stephen Porter, Kristian Taylor, and Leanne ten Brinke, "Memory for Media: Investigation of False Memories for Negatively and Positively Charged Public Events," *Memory* 16, no. 6 (2008): 658–66.

238. *Mississippi Cold Case*, directed by David Ridgen (Toronto: Canadian Broadcasting Corporation, 2007).

239. See, for example, https://en.wikipedia.org/wiki/Mississippi_Summer_Project; Jon Else, *True South: Henry Hampton and "Eyes on the Prize," the Landmark Television Series That Reframed the Civil Rights Movement* (New York: Viking, 2017), 174; and Lee Anna Sherman, *A Small Town Rises: A Sharecropper and a College Girl Join the Struggle for Justice in Shaw, Mississippi* (NP: Bog Lily Press, 2020), 99.

240. David Dennis Jr., "Ahmaud Arbery Will Not Be Erased," *The Atlantic*, July 7, 2020, https://www.atlantamagazine.com/great-reads/ahmaud-arbery-will-not-be-erased/, emphasis in original.

INDEX

United States Commission on Civil Rights, 43
University of California, 47
University of Florida, 92

Van Dyke, Jon, 20, 21, 22
Vicksburg, Mississippi, 48, 67
Vicksburg Evening-Post, 62, 129
Vollers, Maryanne, 78, 139, 141
Voter Education Project (VEP), 13, 131

Walking with the Wind, 91
Walthall County, Mississippi, 24
Washington University, Missouri, 82
Watkins, Hollis, 58, 85, 87, 93, 121
Watson, Bruce, 61, 97, 135
We Are Not Afraid, 78
Webb, Dave, 37, 41, 50, 64, 65, 67
Webb, Mary Lou, 65
Western College for Women (Miami University, Oxford, Ohio), 7, 44, 100, 101, 136

White Citizens' Councils (WCC), 12, 27, 59, 130, 131, 132
Whitehead, Don, 32, 80
Wilkins, Roy, 36
Williams, Marco, 75
Winona, Mississippi, 28
Witness in Philadelphia, 96, 113
Woodville Republican, 50, 62
World War II, 11, 29, 39, 52

Yale Daily News, 19, 20, 23, 27
Yale University, 7, 14, 16, 18, 19, 20, 21, 22, 23, 24, 25, 26, 29, 100, 109
Yazoo City, Mississippi, 21
Yazoo River, 70
Yockanookany River, 92–93
Young, Roger, 100

ABOUT THE AUTHOR

Courtesy of Davis W. Houck

Davis W. Houck is Fannie Lou Hamer Professor of Rhetorical Studies at Florida State University. He is the author or editor of twelve books, including projects on Emmett Till, Fannie Lou Hamer, and the women of the civil rights movement. He is also the founder of the Emmett Till Archive at FSU and is partnering with the West Tallahatchie School District in the Mississippi Delta to bring Till-themed archival documents to high school students.

Also by Davis W. Houck

Emmett Till and the Mississippi Press
Women and the Civil Rights Movement, 1954–1965
The Speeches of Fannie Lou Hamer: To Tell It Like It Is